Collins

Teacher's Guide 1
Vocabulary, Grammar and Punctuation Skills

Author: Abigail Steel

William Collins' dream of knowledge for all began with the publication of his first book in 1819.

A self-educated mill worker, he not only enriched millions of lives, but also founded a flourishing publishing house. Today, staying true to this spirit, Collins books are packed with inspiration, innovation and practical expertise. They place you at the centre of a world of possibility and give you exactly what you need to explore it.

Collins. Freedom to teach.

Published by Collins
An imprint of HarperCollins*Publishers*
The News Building
1 London Bridge Street
London
SE1 9GF

Browse the complete Collins catalogue at
www.collins.co.uk

British Library Cataloguing in Publication Data

A catalogue record for this publication is available from the British Library.

Publishing Director: Lee Newman
Publishing Manager: Helen Doran
Senior Editor: Hannah Dove
Project Manager: Emily Hooton
Author: Abigail Steel
Development Editor: Jessica Marshall
Copy-editor: Tanya Solomons
Proofreader: Tracy Thomas
Cover design and artwork: Amparo Barrera and Ken Vail Graphic Design
Internal design concept: Amparo Barrera
Typesetter: Ken Vail Graphic Design
Illustrations: Alberto Saichann (Beehive Illustration)
Production Controller: Rachel Weaver

Printed and bound by CPI Group (UK) Ltd, Croydon, CR0 4YY

Contents

About Treasure House

Treasure House is a comprehensive and flexible bank of books and online resources for teaching the English curriculum. The Treasure House series offers two different pathways: one covering each English strand discretely (Skills Focus Pathway) and one integrating texts and the strands to create a programme of study (Integrated English Pathway). This Teacher's Guide is part of the Skills Focus Pathway.

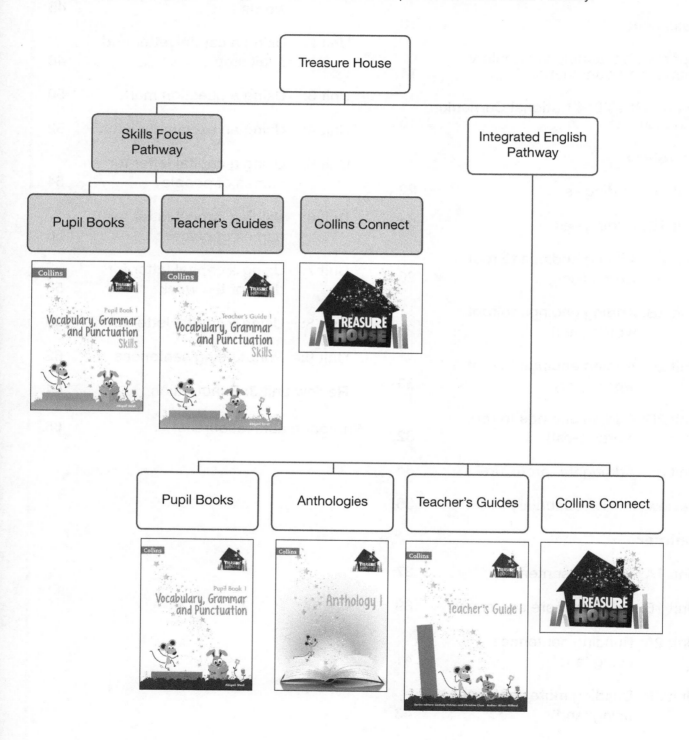

1. Skills Focus

The Skills Focus Pupil Books and Teacher's Guides for all four strands (Comprehension; Spelling; Composition; and Vocabulary, Grammar and Punctuation) allow you to teach each curriculum area in a targeted way. Each unit in the Pupil Book is mapped directly to the statutory requirements of the National Curriculum. Each Teacher's Guide provides step-by-step instructions to guide you through the Pupil Book activities and digital Collins Connect resources for each competency. With a clear focus on skills and clearly-listed curriculum objectives you can select the appropriate resources to support your lessons.

  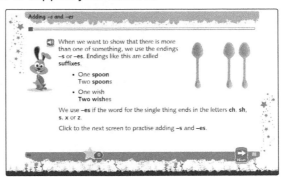

2. Integrated English

Alternatively, the Integrated English pathway offers a complete programme of genre-based teaching sequences. There is one Teacher's Guide and one Anthology for each year group. Each Teacher's Guide provides 15 teaching sequences focused on different genres of text such as fairy tales, letters and newspaper articles. The Anthologies contain the classic texts, fiction, non-fiction and poetry required for each sequence. Each sequence also weaves together all four dimensions of the National Curriculum for English – Comprehension; Spelling; Composition; and Vocabulary, Grammar and Punctuation – into a complete English programme. The Pupil Books and Collins Connect provide targeted explanation of key points and practice activities organised by strand. This programme provides 30 weeks of teaching inspiration.

   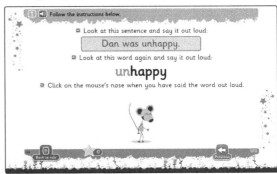

Other components

Handwriting Books, Handwriting Workbooks, Word Books and the online digital resources on Collins Connect are suitable for use with both pathways.

  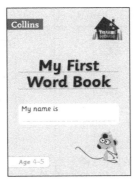

Treasure House Skills Focus Teacher's Guides

Year	Comprehension	Composition	Vocabulary, Grammar and Punctuation	Spelling
1	978-0-00-822290-1	978-0-00-822302-1	978-0-00-822296-3	978-0-00-822308-3
2	978-0-00-822291-8	978-0-00-822303-8	978-0-00-822297-0	978-0-00-822309-0
3	978-0-00-822292-5	978-0-00-822304-5	978-0-00-822298-7	978-0-00-822310-6
4	978-0-00-822293-2	978-0-00-822305-2	978-0-00-822299-4	978-0-00-822311-3
5	978-0-00-822294-9	978-0-00-822306-9	978-0-00-822300-7	978-0-00-822312-0
6	978-0-00-822295-6	978-0-00-822307-6	978-0-00-822301-4	978-0-00-822313-7

Inside the Skills Focus Teacher's Guides

The teaching notes in each unit in the Teacher's Guide provide you with subject information or background, a range of whole class and differentiated activities including photocopiable resource sheets and links to the Pupil Book and the online Collins Connect activities.

Each **Overview** provides clear objectives for each lesson tied into the new curriculum, links to the other relevant components and a list of any additional resources required.

Teaching overview provides a brief introduction to the specific concept or rule and some pointers on how to approach it.

Support, embed & challenge supports a mastery approach with activities provided at three levels.

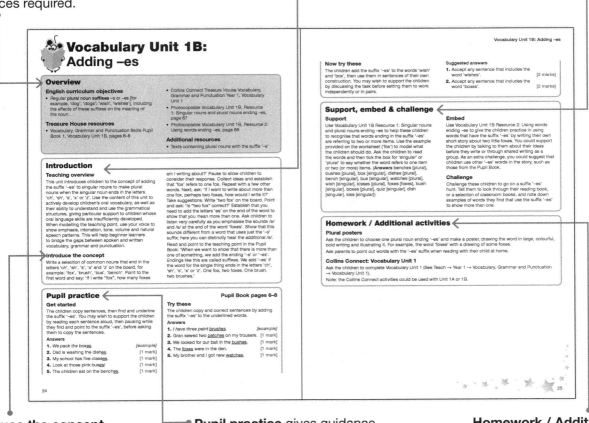

Introduce the concept provides 5–10 minutes of preliminary discussion points or class/group activities to get the pupils engaged in the lesson focus and set out any essential prior learning.

Pupil practice gives guidance and the answers to each of the three sections in the Pupil Book: *Get started*, *Try these* and *Now try these*.

Homework / Additional activities lists ideas for classroom or homework activities, and relevant activities from Collins Connect.

Two photocopiable **resource** worksheets per unit provide extra practice of the specific lesson concept. They are designed to be used with the activities in support, embed or challenge sections.

Treasure House Skills Focus Pupil Books

There are four Skills Focus Pupil Books for each year group, based on the four dimensions of the National Curriculum for English: Comprehension; Spelling; Composition; and Vocabulary, Grammar and Punctuation. The Pupil Books provide a child-friendly introduction to each subject and a range of initial activities for independent pupil-led learning. A Review unit for each term assesses pupils' progress.

Year	Comprehension	Composition	Vocabulary, Grammar and Punctuation	Spelling
1	978-0-00-823634-2	978-0-00-823646-5	978-0-00-823640-3	978-0-00-823652-6
2	978-0-00-823635-9	978-0-00-823647-2	978-0-00-823641-0	978-0-00-823653-3
3	978-0-00-823636-6	978-0-00-823648-9	978-0-00-823642-7	978-0-00-823654-0
4	978-0-00-823637-3	978-0-00-823649-6	978-0-00-823643-4	978-0-00-823655-7
5	978-0-00-823638-0	978-0-00-823650-2	978-0-00-823644-1	978-0-00-823656-4
6	978-0-00-823639-7	978-0-00-823651-9	978-0-00-823645-8	978-0-00-823657-1

Inside the Skills Focus Pupil Books

Comprehension

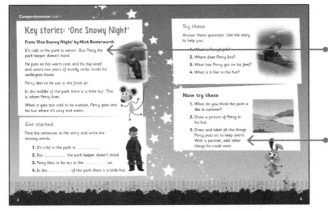

Includes high-quality text extracts covering poetry, prose, traditional tales, playscripts and non-fiction.

Pupils retrieve and record information, learn to draw inferences from texts and increase their familiarity with a wide range of literary genres.

Composition

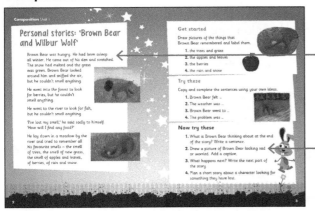

Includes high-quality, annotated text extracts as models for different types of writing.

Children learn how to write effectively and for a purpose.

Vocabulary, Grammar and Punctuation

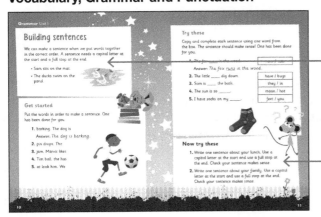

Develops children's knowledge and understanding of grammar and punctuation skills.

A rule is introduced and explained. Children are given lots of opportunities to practise using it.

Spelling

Spelling rules are introduced and explained.

Practice is provided for spotting and using the spelling rules, correcting misspelt words and using the words in context.

Treasure House on Collins Connect

Digital resources for Treasure House are available on Collins Connect which provides a wealth of interactive activities. Treasure House is organised into six core areas on Collins Connect:

- Comprehension
- Spelling
- Composition
- Vocabulary, Grammar and Punctuation
- The Reading Attic
- Teacher's Guides and Anthologies.

For most units in the Skills Focus Pupil Books, there is an accompanying Collins Connect unit focused on the same teaching objective. These fun, independent activities can be used for initial pupil-led learning, or for further practice using a different learning environment. Either way, with Collins Connect, you have a wealth of questions to help children embed their learning.

Treasure House on Collins Connect is available via subscription at connect.collins.co.uk

Features of Treasure House on Collins Connect

The digital resources enhance children's comprehension, spelling, composition, and vocabulary, grammar, punctuation skills through providing:

- a bank of varied and engaging interactive activities so children can practise their skills independently
- audio support to help children access the texts and activities
- auto-mark functionality so children receive instant feedback and have the opportunity to repeat tasks.

Teachers benefit from useful resources and time-saving tools including:

- teacher-facing materials such as audio and explanations for front-of-class teaching or pupil-led learning
- lesson starter videos for some Composition units
- downloadable teaching notes for all online activities
- downloadable teaching notes for Skills Focus and Integrated English pathways
- the option to assign homework activities to your classes
- class records to monitor progress.

Comprehension

- Includes high-quality text extracts covering poetry, prose, traditional tales, playscripts and non-fiction.
- Audio function supports children to access the text and the activities

Composition

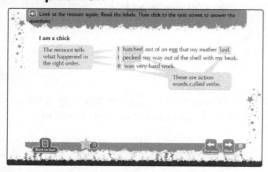

- Activities support children to develop and build more sophisticated sentence structures.
- Every unit ends with a longer piece of writing that can be submitted to the teacher for marking.

Vocabulary, Grammar and Punctuation

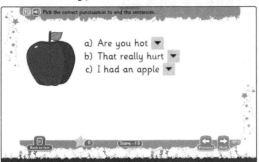

- Fun, practical activities develop children's knowledge and understanding of grammar and punctuation skills.
- Each skill is reinforced with a huge, varied bank of practice questions.

Spelling

- Fun, practical activities develop children's knowledge and understanding of each spelling rule.
- Each rule is reinforced with a huge, varied bank of practice questions.
- Children spell words using an audio prompt, write their own sentences and practise spelling using Look Say Cover Write Check.

Reading Attic

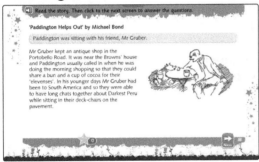

- Children's love of reading is nurtured with texts from exciting children's authors including Michael Bond, David Walliams and Michael Morpurgo.
- Lesson sequences accompany the texts, with drama opportunities and creative strategies for engaging children with key themes, characters and plots.
- Whole-book projects encourage reading for pleasure.

Treasure House Digital Teacher's Guides and Anthologies

The teaching sequences and anthology texts for each year group are included as a flexible bank of resources.

The teaching notes for each skill strand and year group are also included on Collins Connect.

Support, embed and challenge

Treasure House provides comprehensive, detailed differentiation at three levels to ensure that all children are able to access achievement. It is important that children master the basic skills before they go further in their learning. Children may make progress towards the standard at different speeds, with some not reaching it until the very end of the year.

In the Teacher's Guide, Support, Embed and Challenge sections allow teachers to keep the whole class focussed with no child left behind. Two photocopiable resources per unit offer additional material linked to the Support, Embed or Challenge sections.

Support

The Support section offers simpler or more scaffolded activities that will help learners who have not yet grasped specific concepts covered. Background information may also be provided to help children to contextualise learning. This enables children to make progress so that they can keep up with the class.

In Vocabulary, Grammar and Punctuation Teacher's Guides, the activities in the Support section help children to access the rules by giving additional practice of the key teaching point.

If you have a teaching assistant, you may wish to ask him or her to help children work through these activities. You might then ask children who have completed these activities to progress to other more challenging tasks found in the Embed or Challenge sections – or you may decide more practice of the basics is required. Collins Connect can provide further activities.

Embed

The Embed section includes activities to embed learning and is aimed at those who children who are working at the expected standard. It ensures that learners have understood key teaching objectives for the age-group. These activities could be used by the whole class or groups, and most are appropriate for both teacher-led and independent work.

For Vocabulary, Grammar and Punctuation, the activities in Embed enhance children's understanding by offering additional opportunities for the rules to be applied in a variety of contexts.

Challenge

The Challenge section provides additional tasks, questions or activities that will push children who have mastered the concept without difficulty. This keeps children motivated and allows them to gain a greater depth of understanding. You may wish to give these activities to fast finishers to work through independently.

In Vocabulary, Grammar and Punctuation, the challenge activities offer children with the opportunity to work at a higher level by extending the investigation and application of rules to a wider variety of different contexts.

Assessment

Teacher's Guides

There are opportunities for assessment throughout the Treasure House series. The teaching notes in Treasure House Teacher's Guides offer ideas for questions, informal assessment and spelling tests.

Pupil Book Review units

Each Pupil Book has three Review units designed as a quick formative assessment tool for the end of each term. Questions assess the work that has been covered over the previous units. These review units will provide you with an informal way of measuring your pupils' progress. You may wish to use these as Assessment for Learning to help you and your pupils to understand where they are in their learning journey.

The Review units in the Vocabulary, Grammar and Punctuation Pupil Books, include questions testing rules taught in preceding units. By mixing questions on different unit topics within exercises, children can show understanding of multiple rules and patterns.

Assessment in Collins Connect

Activities on Collins Connect can also be used for effective assessment. Activities with auto-marking mean that if children answer incorrectly, they can make another attempt helping them to analyse their own work for mistakes. Homework activities can also be assigned to classes through Collins Connect. At the end of activities, children can select a smiley face to indicate how they found the task giving you useful feedback on any gaps in knowledge.

Class records on Collins Connect allow you to get an overview of children's progress with several features. You can choose to view records by unit, pupil or strand. By viewing detailed scores, you can view pupils' scores question by question in a clear table-format to help you establish areas where there might be particular strengths and weaknesses both class-wide and for individuals.

If you wish, you can also set mastery judgements (mastery achieved and exceeded, mastery achieved, mastery not yet achieved) to help see where your children need more help.

Support with teaching vocabulary, grammar and punctuation

The teacher's guides for Vocabulary, Grammar and Punctuation units can be followed in a simple linear fashion that structures the lesson into four sections:

- assessment of existing skills and knowledge, and an introduction to the unit's teaching point
- completion of the 'pupil practice' questions
- differentiated work, following the Support, Embed and Challenge activity guidance (using the provided photocopiable worksheets)
- homework or additional activities.

However, this lesson structure is intended to be flexible. While we recommend that the first two of these steps should usually be followed in the given order, work following the pupil practice questions can be manipulated in numerous ways to suit the needs, skills and preferences of your class. For example, you may wish to set one of the differentiation activities as homework for the whole class, or to guide children through an 'additional' activity during the lesson, rather than setting it as homework. You may alternatively judge that your class has firmly grasped the concept being taught, and choose not to use any activity suggested, or perhaps introduce only the Extend activity: it is not essential that every activity outlined in the teacher's guide units should be completed.

With the same motivation, many activities (and worksheets) could be adapted for reuse in units other than the one for which they are provided. Several activity and worksheet types are already repeated in similar forms between (and sometimes within) year groups. This is in order both to show the children's changing levels of attainment directly, and to allow any children who have found an activity challenging to reattempt it in a new context after developing their skills.

You may also wish to consider using Support activities in conjunction with the pupil practice questions, if children are struggling with content or a concept with which the Support activity deals. For example, if questions within the 'Try these' and 'Now try these' sections of pupil practice require understanding of adverbials, you may wish to intervene and prepare children using an appropriate Support activity.

By using the teacher's guide units and their suggested activities flexibly, you can choose to tailor the resources at your fingertips to provide the most beneficial learning system for the children being taught. Having confidence in English vocabulary, grammar and punctuation prepares children to function effectively in society as they mature. The aim therefore is to equip children with a strong command of the spoken and written word.

We can make learning vocabulary, grammar and punctuation easy and fun by employing simple techniques to guide children along their literacy journey.

Vocabulary: Establish an ethos in your classroom where words are 'cool'. Talk about your desire to use words that are not the biggest, or the fanciest, or the most complex but that are the 'right words for the job'. Try not to make assumptions about children's level of vocabulary, sometimes those that have a wide vocabulary do not always know the right times to use it. Consider introducing a word of the week, or word of the day. Mention new, unusual or effective words when reading any text in a natural way, for example, say: 'Oh, what a great word I must remember to use that sometime'. Ensure children are so familiar with using dictionaries and thesaurus's that it becomes second nature for them to use them efficiently when reading and writing.

Grammar: Grammar can be tricky to learn and to teach, especially with primary aged children. Explain to them that having a solid working knowledge of grammar enables them to control their spoken and written words in a way that they can influence and affect their reader effectively. Sometimes the very best authors use their knowledge of grammar rules to break them and create interesting effects! Try to make grammar as simple as possible whilst giving enough explanation to be memorable and logical. Repetition is important to help children embed elements of grammar. Another important aspect is demonstrating grammar in real life contexts so children can experience how and why it is needed. A fun activity can be to show the wrong grammar in modeled sentences on the board. This also demonstrates to children how much grammar they have already picked up through their daily use of language, both spoken and written.

Punctuation: Punctuation is generally more straightforward to get to grips with but it does require lots of repetition for children to remember to use it correctly! You can talk to children incidentally about any punctuation marks they come across in wider literature at the same time as focusing on a few aspects at a time through your planned teaching. Model examples of writing with and without punctuation marks to help children notice the different effects.

Delivering the 2014 National Curriculum for English

Unit	Title	Treasure House resources	Collins Connect	English Programme of Study	KS1 English Grammar, Punctuation and Spelling Test code
Vocabulary					
1A	Adding –s	• Vocabulary, Grammar and Punctuation Skills Pupil Book 1, Vocabulary Unit 1A, pages 4–5 • Vocabulary, Grammar and Punctuation Skills Teacher's Guide 1 – Vocabulary Unit 1A, pages 22–23 – Photocopiable Vocabulary Unit 1A, Resource 1: Adding –s, page 65 – Photocopiable Vocabulary Unit 1A, Resource 2: Plural nouns with the suffix –s, page 66	Treasure House Vocabulary, Grammar and Punctuation Year 1, Vocabulary Unit 1	Regular plural noun suffixes –s or –es [for example, dog, dogs; wish, wishes], including the effects of these suffixes on the meaning of the noun	G6.3
1B	Adding –es	• Vocabulary, Grammar and Punctuation Skills Pupil Book 1, Vocabulary Unit 1B, pages 6–7 • Vocabulary, Grammar and Punctuation Skills Teacher's Guide 1 – Vocabulary Unit 1B, pages 24–25 – Photocopiable Vocabulary Unit 1B, Resource 1: Singular nouns and plural nouns ending –es, page 67 – Photocopiable Vocabulary Unit 1B, Resource 2: Using words ending –es, page 68	Treasure House Vocabulary, Grammar and Punctuation Year 1, Vocabulary Unit 1	Regular plural noun suffixes –s or –es [for example, dog, dogs; wish, wishes], including the effects of these suffixes on the meaning of the noun	G6.3
2A	Adding endings to root words (–ing)	• Vocabulary, Grammar and Punctuation Skills Pupil Book 1, Vocabulary Unit 2A, pages 8–9 • Vocabulary, Grammar and Punctuation Skills Teacher's Guide 1 – Vocabulary Unit 2A, pages 26–27 – Photocopiable Vocabulary Unit 2A, Resource 1: Adding –ing to verbs, page 69 – Photocopiable Vocabulary Unit 2A, Resource 2: Using verbs ending –ing, page 70	Treasure House Vocabulary, Grammar and Punctuation Year 1, Vocabulary Unit 2	Suffixes that can be added to verbs where no change is needed in the spelling of root words (e.g. helping, helped, helper)	G6.3

Unit	Title	Treasure House resources	Collins Connect	English Programme of Study	KS1 English Grammar, Punctuation and Spelling Test code
2B	Adding endings to root words (–ed)	• Vocabulary, Grammar and Punctuation Skills Pupil Book 1, Vocabulary Unit 2B, pages 10–11 • Vocabulary, Grammar and Punctuation Skills Teacher's Guide 1 – Vocabulary Unit 2B, pages 28–29 – Photocopiable Vocabulary Unit 2B, Resource 1: Adding –ed to verbs, page 71 – Photocopiable Vocabulary Unit 2B, Resource 2: Past or future tense? page 72	Treasure House Vocabulary, Grammar and Punctuation Year 1, Vocabulary Unit 2	Suffixes that can be added to verbs where no change is needed in the spelling of root words (e.g. helping, helped, helper)	G6.3
2C	Adding endings to root words (–er)	• Vocabulary, Grammar and Punctuation Skills Pupil Book 1, Vocabulary Unit 2C, pages 12–13 • Vocabulary, Grammar and Punctuation Skills Teacher's Guide 1 – Vocabulary Unit 2C, pages 30–31 – Photocopiable Vocabulary Unit 2C, Resource 1: Using adjectives to compare, page 73 – Photocopiable Vocabulary Unit 2C, Resource 2: About me, page 74	Treasure House Vocabulary, Grammar and Punctuation Year 1, Vocabulary Unit 2	Suffixes that can be added to verbs [and adjectives] where no change is needed in the spelling of root words (e.g. helping, helped, helper)	G6.3
2D	Adding endings to root words (–est)	• Vocabulary, Grammar and Punctuation Skills Pupil Book 1, Vocabulary Unit 2D, pages 14–15 • Vocabulary, Grammar and Punctuation Skills Teacher's Guide 1 – Vocabulary Unit 2D, pages 32–33 – Photocopiable Vocabulary Unit 2D, Resource 1: Rosettes, page 75 – Photocopiable Vocabulary Unit 2D, Resource 2: Labels, page 76	Treasure House Vocabulary, Grammar and Punctuation Year 1, Vocabulary Unit 2	Suffixes that can be added to verbs [and adjectives] where no change is needed in the spelling of root words (e.g. helping, helped, helper)	G6.3

Unit	Title	Treasure House resources	Collins Connect	English Programme of Study	KS1 English Grammar, Punctuation and Spelling Test code
3	Adding the prefix un–	• Vocabulary, Grammar and Punctuation Skills Pupil Book 1, Vocabulary Unit 3, pages 16–17 • Vocabulary, Grammar and Punctuation Skills Teacher's Guide 1 – Vocabulary Unit 3, pages 34–35 – Photocopiable Vocabulary Unit 3, Resource 1: Adding un–, page 77 – Photocopiable Vocabulary Unit 3, Resource 2: Word search, page 78	Treasure House Vocabulary, Grammar and Punctuation Year 1, Vocabulary Unit 3	How the prefix un– changes the meaning of verbs and adjectives [negation, for example, unkind, or undoing: untie the boat]	G6.2
Grammar					
1A	Building sentences	• Vocabulary, Grammar and Punctuation Skills Pupil Book 1, Grammar Unit 1A, pages 20–21 • Vocabulary, Grammar and Punctuation Skills Teacher's Guide 1 – Grammar Unit 1A, pages 37–38 – Photocopiable Grammar Unit 1A, Resource 1: Making sentences, page 79 – Photocopiable Grammar Unit 1A, Resource 2: Building your own sentences, page 80	Treasure House Vocabulary, Grammar and Punctuation Year 1, Grammar Unit 1	How words can combine to make sentences	G3.1
1B	Building more sentences	• Vocabulary, Grammar and Punctuation Skills Pupil Book 1, Grammar Unit 1B, pages 22–23 • Vocabulary, Grammar and Punctuation Skills Teacher's Guide 1 – Grammar Unit 1B, pages 39–40 – Photocopiable Grammar Unit 1B, Resource 1: Is it a sentence? page 81 – Photocopiable Grammar Unit 1B, Resource 2: Finishing sentences, page 82	Treasure House Vocabulary, Grammar and Punctuation Year 1, Grammar Unit 1	How words can combine to make sentences	G3.1

Unit	Title	Treasure House resources	Collins Connect	English Programme of Study	KS1 English Grammar, Punctuation and Spelling Test code
2A	Building sentences using 'and'	• Vocabulary, Grammar and Punctuation Skills Pupil Book 1, Grammar Unit 2A, pages 24–25 • Vocabulary, Grammar and Punctuation Skills Teacher's Guide 1 – Grammar Unit 2A, pages 41–42 – Photocopiable Grammar Unit 2A, Resource 1: Joining sentences, page 83 – Photocopiable Grammar Unit 2A, Resource 2: Building sentences using 'and', page 84	Treasure House Vocabulary, Grammar and Punctuation Year 1, Grammar Unit 2	Joining words and joining clauses using and	G3.3
2B	Building more sentences using 'and'	• Vocabulary, Grammar and Punctuation Skills Pupil Book 1, Grammar Unit 2B, pages 26–27 • Vocabulary, Grammar and Punctuation Skills Teacher's Guide 1 – Grammar Unit 2B, pages 43–44 – Photocopiable Grammar Unit 2B, Resource 1: Is it a sentence? page 85 – Photocopiable Grammar Unit 2B, Resource 2: Completing sentences using 'but', page 86	Treasure House Vocabulary, Grammar and Punctuation Year 1, Grammar Unit 2	Joining words and joining clauses using and	G3.3
Punctuation					
1	Leaving spaces between words	• Vocabulary, Grammar and Punctuation Skills Pupil Book 1, Punctuation Unit 1, pages 30–31 • Vocabulary, Grammar and Punctuation Skills Teacher's Guide 1 – Punctuation Unit 1, pages 46–47 – Photocopiable Punctuation Unit 1, Resource 1: Word snakes, page 87 – Photocopiable Punctuation Unit 1, Resource 2: Spaces between words, page 88		Separation of words with spaces	

Unit	Title	Treasure House resources	Collins Connect	English Programme of Study	KS1 English Grammar, Punctuation and Spelling Test code

2	Using a capital letter and a full stop	• Vocabulary, Grammar and Punctuation Skills Pupil Book 1, Punctuation Unit 2, pages 32–33
		• Vocabulary, Grammar and Punctuation Skills Teacher's Guide 1
		  – Punctuation Unit 2, pages 48–49
		  – Photocopiable Punctuation Unit 2, Resource 1: Matching letters, page 89
		  – Photocopiable Punctuation Unit 2, Resource 2: Writing capital letters, page 90
				Introduction to capital letters, full stops, question marks and exclamation marks to demarcate sentences	G5.1
					G5.2
					G5.3
					G5.4

3	Using a question mark	• Vocabulary, Grammar and Punctuation Skills Pupil Book 1, Punctuation Unit 3, pages 34–35
		• Vocabulary, Grammar and Punctuation Skills Teacher's Guide 1
		  – Punctuation Unit 3, pages 50–51
		  – Photocopiable Punctuation Unit 3, Resource 1: Adding question marks, page 91
		  – Photocopiable Punctuation Unit 3, Resource 2: Matching questions and answers, page 92
				Introduction to capital letters, full stops, question marks and exclamation marks to demarcate sentences	G5.1
					G5.2
					G5.3
					G5.4

4	Using an exclamation mark	• Vocabulary, Grammar and Punctuation Skills Pupil Book 1, Punctuation Unit 4, pages 36–37
		• Vocabulary, Grammar and Punctuation Skills Teacher's Guide 1
		  – Punctuation Unit 4, pages 52–53
		  – Photocopiable Punctuation Unit 4, Resource 1: Adding exclamation marks and question marks, page 93
		  – Photocopiable Punctuation Unit 4, Resource 2: Exclamations, page 94
				Introduction to capital letters, full stops, question marks and exclamation marks to demarcate sentences	G5.1
					G5.2
					G5.3
					G5.4

Unit	Title	Treasure House resources	Collins Connect	English Programme of Study	KS1 English Grammar, Punctuation and Spelling Test code

5	Using a capital letter for names of people	• Vocabulary, Grammar and Punctuation Skills Pupil Book 1, Punctuation Unit 5, pages 38–39
		• Vocabulary, Grammar and Punctuation Skills Teacher's Guide 1
		  – Punctuation Unit 5, pages 54–55
		  – Photocopiable Punctuation Unit 5, Resource 1: Capital letters for people's names, page 95
		  – Photocopiable Punctuation Unit 5, Resource 2: Pet names, page 96
			Treasure House Vocabulary, Grammar and Punctuation Year 1, Punctuation Unit 2	Using a capital letter for names of people, places, the days of the week, and the personal pronoun 'I'	G5.1

6	Using a capital letter for names of places	• Vocabulary, Grammar and Punctuation Skills Pupil Book 1, Punctuation Unit 6, pages 40–41
		• Vocabulary, Grammar and Punctuation Skills Teacher's Guide 1
		  – Punctuation Unit 6, pages 56–57
		  – Photocopiable Punctuation Unit 6, Resource 1: Place names, page 97
		  – Photocopiable Punctuation Unit 6, Resource 2: Fact file, page 98
			Treasure House Vocabulary, Grammar and Punctuation Year 1, Punctuation Unit 3	Using a capital letter for names of people, places, the days of the week, and the personal pronoun 'I'	G5.1

7	Using a capital letter for days of the week	• Vocabulary, Grammar and Punctuation Skills Pupil Book 1, Punctuation Unit 7, pages 42–43
		• Vocabulary, Grammar and Punctuation Skills Teacher's Guide 1
		  – Punctuation Unit 7, pages 58–59
		  – Photocopiable Punctuation Unit 7, Resource 1: Days of the week word search, page 99
		  – Photocopiable Punctuation Unit 7, Resource 2: Months of the year, page 100
			Treasure House Vocabulary, Grammar and Punctuation Year 1, Punctuation Unit 3	Using a capital letter for names of people, places, the days of the week, and the personal pronoun 'I'	G5.1

Unit	Title	Treasure House resources	Collins Connect	English Programme of Study	KS1 English Grammar, Punctuation and Spelling Test code

8	Using a capital letter for 'I'	• Vocabulary, Grammar and Punctuation Skills Pupil Book 1, Punctuation Unit 8, pages 44–45
		• Vocabulary, Grammar and Punctuation Skills Teacher's Guide 1
		  – Punctuation Unit 8, pages 60–61
		  – Photocopiable Punctuation Unit 8, Resource 1: Using a capital I, page 101
		  – Photocopiable Punctuation Unit 8, Resource 2: All about me, page 102
			Treasure House Vocabulary, Grammar and Punctuation Year 1, Punctuation Unit 2	Using a capital letter for names of people, places, the days of the week, and the personal pronoun 'I'	G5.1

9	Punctuating sentences	• Vocabulary, Grammar and Punctuation Skills Pupil Book 1, Punctuation Unit 9, pages 46–47
		• Vocabulary, Grammar and Punctuation Skills Teacher's Guide 1
		  – Punctuation Unit 9, pages 62–63
		  – Photocopiable Punctuation Unit 9, Resource 1: End of sentence punctuation, page 103
		  – Photocopiable Punctuation Unit 9, Resource 2: Correcting sentences, page 104
			Treasure House Vocabulary, Grammar and Punctuation Year 1, Punctuation Unit 1	Introduction to capital letters, full stops, question marks and exclamation marks to demarcate sentences
				
				Using a capital letter for names of people, places, the days of the week, and the personal pronoun 'I'
					G5.1
					G5.2
					G5.3
					G5.4

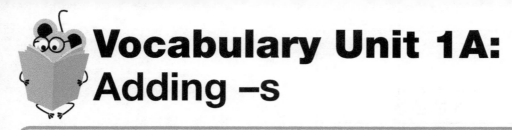

Vocabulary Unit 1A: Adding –s

Overview

English curriculum objectives

- Regular **plural noun suffixes** –s or –es [for example, 'dog', 'dogs'; 'wish', 'wishes'], including the effects of these suffixes on the meaning of the noun

Treasure House resources

- Vocabulary, Grammar and Punctuation Skills Pupil Book 1, Vocabulary Unit 1A, pages 4–5

- Collins Connect Treasure House Vocabulary, Grammar and Punctuation Year 1, Vocabulary Unit 1
- Photocopiable Vocabulary Unit 1A, Resource 1: Adding –s, page 65
- Photocopiable Vocabulary Unit 1A, Resource 2: Plural nouns with the suffix –s, page 66

Additional resources

- Texts containing plural nouns with the suffix '–s'

Introduction

Teaching overview

This unit introduces children to the concept of adding the suffix '–s' when we want to show that there is more than one of something. Use the content of this unit to actively develop children's oral vocabulary as well as their ability to understand and use the grammatical structures, giving particular support to children whose oral language skills are insufficiently developed. When modelling the teaching point, use your voice to show emphasis, intonation, tone, volume and natural speech patterns. This will help beginner learners to bridge the gaps between spoken and written vocabulary, grammar and punctuation.

Introduce the concept

Write a selection of common nouns on the board, for example: 'chair', 'ball', 'sock', 'girl', 'boy'. Point to the first word and say: 'If I write "chair", how many chairs am I writing about?' Pause to allow the children to consider their response. Collect ideas and establish that 'chair' refers to one chair. Repeat with a few other words.

Then ask: 'If I want to write about more than one chair, perhaps two chairs, how would I write it?' Take suggestions. Write 'two chair' on the board. Point and ask: 'Is "two chair" correct?' Establish that you need to add a letter 's' to the end of the word to show that you mean more than one.

Read and point to the teaching point in the Pupil Book: 'When we want to show that there is more than one of something, we usually add '–s'. An added ending like this is called a suffix. One cat, two cats. One boy, two boys.' You may wish to emphasise that the suffix '–s' sometimes sounds like a /z/ (as in 'boys') so point out to the children that this can be tricky for spelling.

Pupil practice

Pupil Book pages 4–5

Get started

The children copy sentences, then find and underline the suffix '–s'. You may wish to support the children by reading each sentence aloud, then pausing while they find and point to the suffix '–s', before asking them to copy the sentences.

Answers

1. *My cats are black.* [example]
2. I read three books. [1 mark]
3. I saw some chicks in a nest. [1 mark]
4. The children played with the toys. [1 mark]
5. I used pens to colour my picture. [1 mark]

Try these

The children copy and correct sentences by adding the suffix '–s' to the underlined words.

Answers

1. *I put my socks on my feet.* [example]
2. We lined up all the red toy trains. [1 mark]
3. All my pens had run out of ink. [1 mark]
4. The teacher told us to put our coats on. [1 mark]
5. I have six books. [1 mark]

Now try these

The children add the suffix '–s' to the words 'gift' and 'bag', then use them in sentences of their own construction. You may wish to support the children by discussing the task before setting them to work independently or in pairs.

Suggested answers

1. Accept any sentence that includes the word 'gifts'. [2 marks]
2. Accept any sentence that includes the word 'bags'. [2 marks]

Support, embed & challenge

Support

Use Vocabulary Unit 1A Resource 1: Adding –s to give these children practice in recognising whether the suffix '–s' is needed. Either ask the children to read the sentences, or read them aloud together to emphasise how they sound without the suffix '–s'. Ask the children to decide whether the suffix '–s' is needed in each sentence and tick 'yes' or 'no'. Then ask children to write the 's' in the gap if needed. (**Answers** There are two pillows on my bed. [yes]; Three cats live next door to me. [yes]; Mum gave me a new pencil. [no]; I picked four apples. [yes])

Embed

Use Vocabulary Unit 1A Resource 2: Plural nouns with the suffix –s to provide the children with practice in writing plural nouns that require the suffix '–s'. Ask the children to look at the example on the worksheet ('one spoon, two spoons'). Ask them to read each phrase in the left column and draw a picture of what it says. Then, ask them to read the number in the right column and write the correct plural noun (by adding the suffix '–s' to the singular noun given) before drawing a picture to show what it refers to. (**Answers** three frogs, four birds, five cars, six flowers)

Challenge

Challenge these children to go on a suffix '–s' hunt. Tell them to look through their reading book, or a selection of classroom books, and note down examples of words they find that use the suffix '–s' to show more than one.

Homework / Additional activities

Seeing double

Ask the children to make a list of things that they have more than one of, for example: 'two socks', 'two eyes', 'two ears', 'two shoes'.

Collins Connect: Vocabulary Unit 1

Ask the children to complete Vocabulary Unit 1 (See Teach → Year 1 → Vocabulary, Grammar and Punctuation → Vocabulary Unit 1).

Note: the Collins Connect activities could be used with Unit 1A or 1B.

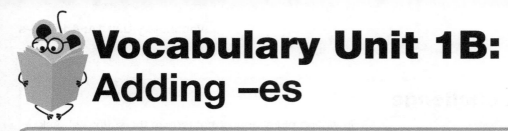

Vocabulary Unit 1B: Adding –es

Overview

English curriculum objectives

- Regular plural noun **suffixes** –s or –es [for example, 'dog', 'dogs'; 'wish', 'wishes'], including the effects of these suffixes on the meaning of the noun

Treasure House resources

- Vocabulary, Grammar and Punctuation Skills Pupil Book 1, Vocabulary Unit 1B, pages 6–8

- Collins Connect Treasure House Vocabulary, Grammar and Punctuation Year 1, Vocabulary Unit 1
- Photocopiable Vocabulary Unit 1B, Resource 1: Singular nouns and plural nouns ending –es, page 67
- Photocopiable Vocabulary Unit 1B, Resource 2: Using words ending –es, page 68

Additional resources

- Texts containing plural nouns with the suffix '–s'

Introduction

Teaching overview

This unit introduces children to the concept of adding the suffix '–es' to singular nouns to make plural nouns when the singular noun ends in the letters 'ch', 'sh', 's', 'x' or 'z'. Use the content of this unit to actively develop children's oral vocabulary, as well as their ability to understand and use the grammatical structures, giving particular support to children whose oral language skills are insufficiently developed. When modelling the teaching point, use your voice to show emphasis, intonation, tone, volume and natural speech patterns. This will help beginner learners to bridge the gaps between spoken and written vocabulary, grammar and punctuation.

Introduce the concept

Write a selection of common nouns that end in the letters 'ch', 'sh', 's', 'x' and 'z' on the board, for example: 'fox', 'brush', 'bus', 'bench'. Point to the first word and say: 'If I write "fox", how many foxes

am I writing about?' Pause to allow children to consider their response. Collect ideas and establish that 'fox' refers to one fox. Repeat with a few other words. Next, ask: 'If I want to write about more than one fox, perhaps two foxes, how would I write it?' Take suggestions. Write 'two fox' on the board. Point and ask: 'Is "two fox" correct?' Establish that you need to add the letters 'es' on the end of the word to show that you mean more than one. Ask children to listen very carefully as you emphasise the sounds /e/ and /s/ at the end of the word 'foxes'. Show that this sounds different from a word that uses just the '–s' suffix; here you can distinctly hear the additional /e/.

Read and point to the teaching point in the Pupil Book: 'When we want to show that there is more than one of something, we add the ending '–s' or '–es'. Endings like this are called suffixes. We add '–es' if the word for the single thing ends in the letters 'ch', 'sh', 's', 'x' or 'z'. One fox, two foxes. One brush, two brushes.'

Pupil practice

Pupil Book pages 6–8

Get started

The children copy sentences, then find and underline the suffix '–es'. You may wish to support the children by reading each sentence aloud, then pausing while they find and point to the suffix '–es', before asking them to copy the sentences.

Answers

1. *We pack the box*es.   *[example]*
2. Dad is washing the dish*es*.   [1 mark]
3. My school has five class*es*.   [1 mark]
4. Look at those pink bus*es*!   [1 mark]
5. The children sat on the bench*es*.   [1 mark]

Try these

The children copy and correct sentences by adding the suffix '–es' to the underlined words.

Answers

1. *I have three paint <u>brushes</u>.*   *[example]*
2. Gran sewed two <u>patches</u> on my trousers. [1 mark]
3. We looked for our ball in the <u>bushes</u>.   [1 mark]
4. The <u>foxes</u> were in the den.   [1 mark]
5. My brother and I got new <u>watches</u>.   [1 mark]

Now try these

The children add the suffix '–es' to the words 'wish' and 'box', then use them in sentences of their own construction. You may wish to support the children by discussing the task before setting them to work independently or in pairs.

Suggested answers

1. Accept any sentence that includes the word 'wishes'. [2 marks]

2. Accept any sentence that includes the word 'boxes'. [2 marks]

Support, embed & challenge

Support

Use Vocabulary Unit 1B Resource 1: Singular nouns and plural nouns ending –es to help these children to recognise that words ending in the suffix '–es' are referring to two or more items. Use the example provided on the worksheet ('fox') to model what the children should do. Ask the children to read the words and then tick the box for 'singular' or 'plural' to say whether the word refers to one item or two (or more) items. (**Answers** benches [plural], bushes [plural], box [singular], dishes [plural], bench [singular], bus [singular], watches [plural], wish [singular], kisses [plural], foxes [foxes], bush [singular], boxes [plural], quiz [singular], dish [singular], kiss [singular])

Embed

Use Vocabulary Unit 1B Resource 2: Using words ending –es to give the children practice in using words that have the suffix '–es' by writing their own short story about two little foxes. You could support the children by talking to them about their ideas before they write or through shared writing as a group. As an extra challenge, you could suggest that children use other '–es' words in the story, such as those from the Pupil Book.

Challenge

Challenge these children to go on a suffix '–es' hunt. Tell them to look through their reading book, or a selection of classroom books, and note down examples of words they find that use the suffix '–es' to show more than one.

Homework / Additional activities

Plural posters

Ask the children to choose one plural noun ending '–es' and make a poster, drawing the word in large, colourful, bold writing and illustrating it. For example, the word 'foxes' with a drawing of some foxes.

Ask parents to point out words with the '–es' suffix when reading with their child at home.

Collins Connect: Vocabulary Unit 1

Ask the children to complete Vocabulary Unit 1 (See Teach → Year 1 → Vocabulary, Grammar and Punctuation → Vocabulary Unit 1).

Note: the Collins Connect activities could be used with Unit 1A or 1B.

Vocabulary Unit 2A: Adding endings to root words (–ing)

Overview

English curriculum objectives
- **Suffixes** that can be added to **verbs** where no change is needed in the spelling of root words (e.g. 'helping', 'helped', 'helper')

Treasure House resources
- Vocabulary, Grammar and Punctuation Skills Pupil Book 1, Vocabulary Unit 2A, pages 8–9

- Collins Connect Treasure House Vocabulary, Grammar and Punctuation Year 1, Vocabulary Unit 2
- Photocopiable Vocabulary Unit 2A, Resource 1: Adding –ing to verbs, page 69
- Photocopiable Vocabulary Unit 2A, Resource 2: Using verbs ending –ing, page 70

Additional resources
- Pictures of things performing actions

Introduction

Teaching overview

The basic form of a verb is called the infinitive, which is usually used with the word 'to', as in 'I like to walk' or 'he needs to think'. Verbs change form according to the tense and person they express. The verb form that ends in '–ing' is the present participle. Present participles are used to form continuous tenses, as in 'I am running' or 'she was reading'. Verbs ending '–ing' are also used as gerunds (nouns formed from verbs denoting actions, processes or states) and can function as adjectives, for example 'a beaming smile' or 'a piercing shriek'. This unit focuses on adding the suffix '–ing' to verbs without needing to change the spelling of the root verb. Use the content of this unit to actively develop children's oral vocabulary as well as their ability to understand and use the grammatical structures, giving particular support to children whose oral language skills are insufficiently developed. When modelling the teaching point, use your voice to show emphasis, intonation, tone, volume and natural speech patterns. This will help beginner learners to bridge the gaps between spoken and written vocabulary, grammar and punctuation.

Introduce the concept

Show or draw pictures of people and things performing actions, for example people walking,

playing and eating. (Avoid including pictures of actions where the root verbs that describe them are changed when '–ing' is added, such as 'swimming', 'running' and 'baking'.) Ask the children what the people or things are doing in each picture, prompting the children (if necessary) to give you the present participle, for example: 'They are walking.' 'It is listening.' 'She is talking.' Write the participles on the board, for example: 'walking', 'flying', 'seeing'. Ask: 'What sort of words are these?' Elicit that they are verbs (or doing words). Underline the infinitive in each example on the board. Tell the children that these are the original root verbs and say each infinitive, for example: 'walk', 'play', 'eat', 'listen', 'talk', 'fly', 'see', 'sleep', 'float'. Point to the '–ing' endings and tell the children that this is the suffix '–ing'. Ask the children what a suffix is and establish that it is an ending that can be added to words to change or add to their original meaning. Explain that, when '–ing' is added to verbs, it means that the action is continuous: it continues happening. Point out that the things in the pictures are all in the middle of happening. Tell the children that there is usually no change in spelling to the original verb when '–ing' is added to the end.

Read and point to the teaching point in the Pupil Book: 'We can change words by adding the ending '–ing'. An ending like this is called a suffix. The farmer was milking his cow. I was drawing a picture.'

Pupil practice

Pupil Book pages 8–9

Get started

The children copy sentences, then find and underline the suffix '–ing'. You may wish to support the children by reading each sentence aloud, then pausing while they find and point to the suffix '–ing', before asking them to copy the sentences.

Answers

1. *Dad was sleeping in his chair.*   [example]
2. Mum was talking on the phone.   [1 mark]
3. My brother was playing with his toys.   [1 mark]
4. The lamp is glowing.   [1 mark]
5. I keep yawning!   [1 mark]

Try these

The children copy and correct sentences by adding the suffix '–ing' to the underlined words.

Answers

1. *I am eating my dinner.*   [example]

2. Dad is painting the wall.   [1 mark]

3. Katya is looking at her book.   [1 mark]

4. We were climbing the tree.   [1 mark]

5. We have been walking to school
every day.   [1 mark]

Now try these

The children add the suffix '–ing' to the words 'paint' and 'play', then use them in sentences of their own construction. You may wish to support the children by discussing the task before setting them to work independently or in pairs.

Suggested answers

1. Accept any sentence that includes
the word 'painting'.   [2 marks]

2. Accept any sentence that includes
the word 'playing'.   [2 marks]

Support, embed & challenge

Support

Use Vocabulary Unit 2A Resource 1: Adding –ing to verbs to provide these children with practice in reading, writing and understanding words that end in '–ing' but do not need changes made to the root word when the suffix is added. Ask the children to read the word sums and write the new words. Use the resource sheet to discuss the spellings, pronunciations and meanings of the words. Extend the task by asking the children to put some of the words into sentences, either orally or written. (**Answers** 1. *milking [example]*, 2. drawing, 3. sleeping, 4. talking, 5. asking, 6. thinking, 7. meeting, 8. throwing)

Embed

Use Vocabulary Unit 2A Resource 2: Using verbs ending –ing to encourage the children to use '–ing'

words by choosing and inserting the correct one from the box into each sentence. Read through the sentences together and model how the children could try inserting each one until they find the correct one. This is an amusing way to practise thinking about the meanings of the words as the children will test silly sentences such as 'I enjoyed throwing a picture.' (**Answers** 1. We had fun climbing the tree. 2. The film kept us laughing all day. 3. The teacher was reading a story. 4. I enjoyed drawing a picture. 5. He was watching the show. 6. We were throwing and catching the ball. Accept other word choices if they are appropriate.)

Challenge

Challenge these children to add the suffix '–ing' to the following words and then use each word in a sentence of their own construction: 'mark', 'cook', 'scratch', 'follow', 'pick', 'sew', 'squash', 'jump'.

Homework / Additional activities

Parent-ing

Ask the children to talk to their parents about words that end in the '–ing' suffix. Ask parents to help their children by writing down any '–ing' words they encounter during home reading that don't require any change in spelling when the '–ing' ending is added to the root word.

Collins Connect: Vocabulary Unit 2

Ask the children to complete Vocabulary Unit 2 (See Teach → Year 1 → Vocabulary, Grammar and Punctuation → Vocabulary Unit 2).

Note: the Collins Connect activities could be used with Unit 2A, 2B, 2C and 2D.

Vocabulary Unit 2B: Adding endings to root words (–ed)

Overview

English curriculum objectives
- **Suffixes** that can be added to **verbs** where no change is needed in the spelling of root words (e.g. 'helping', 'helped', 'helper')

Treasure House resources
- Vocabulary, Grammar and Punctuation Skills Pupil Book 1, Vocabulary Unit 2B, pages 10–11

- Collins Connect Treasure House Vocabulary, Grammar and Punctuation Year 1, Vocabulary Unit 2
- Photocopiable Vocabulary Unit 2B, Resource 1: Adding –ed to verbs, page 71
- Photocopiable Vocabulary Unit 2B, Resource 2: Past or future tense? page 72

Introduction

Teaching overview

The basic form of a verb is called the infinitive, which is usually used with the word 'to', as in 'we like to talk' or 'that's good to know'. Verbs change form according to the tense and person they express. To refer to things that have already happened, past participles and past tense verbs are, in most cases, formed by adding '–ed' to infinitive verbs. Past participles are used to form perfect tenses (for example 'I have joked', 'I had asked', 'I will have talked') and the passive voice, and many of them can be used as adjectives (for example 'bored', 'tiered', 'shocked'). This unit focuses on adding the suffix '–ed' to verbs without needing to change the spelling of the root verb. Use the content of this unit to actively develop children's oral vocabulary as well as their ability to understand and use the grammatical structures, giving particular support to children whose oral language skills are insufficiently developed. When modelling the teaching point, use your voice to show emphasis, intonation, tone, volume and natural speech patterns. This will help beginner learners to bridge the gaps between spoken and written vocabulary, grammar and punctuation.

Introduce the concept

Write a selection of simple verbs on the board, for example: 'wait', 'paint', 'add', 'laugh', 'wash'. Point to the words, read them aloud and say: 'These words are all things that people can do. We can call them "doing words" or the proper name is "verbs". If we want to write about something that somebody has already done, perhaps they did it yesterday or this morning, we need to add an "–ed" suffix to the end of these verbs.' Write on the board: 'wash', 'washed'. Ask: 'If I just write "I wash my face" will the reader know when I washed?' Elicit that this sentence does not specify a time that you wash your face. Say: 'If I write "I washed my face", the reader will know that the washing has already happened; it's in the past. So, the "–ed" ending helps us to know that somebody has already done the action.'

Model adding an '–ed' suffix to the other words you have already written on the board and then read them aloud, emphasising the '–ed' ending. Work with the children to use the verbs with '–ed' endings in simple sentences or phrases.

Read and point to the teaching point in the Pupil Book: 'We can change words by adding the ending '–ed'. An ending like this is called a suffix. I waited for the bus. I painted a picture.'

Pupil practice

Pupil Book pages 10–11

Get started

The children copy sentences, then find and underline the suffix '–ed'. You may wish to support the children by reading each sentence aloud, then pausing while they find and point to the suffix '–ed', before asking them to copy the sentences.

Answers

1. *I add<u>ed</u> one extra sweet to the bag.* [example]
2. Samir need<u>ed</u> to finish his task. [1 mark]
3. I show<u>ed</u> Mum how to play the game. [1 mark]
4. We laugh<u>ed</u> at the funny cartoon. [1 mark]
5. Mum wash<u>ed</u> my dirty socks. [1 mark]

Try these

The children copy and correct sentences by adding the suffix '–ed' to the underlined words.

Answers

1. *Dad <u>painted</u> the wall.* [example]
2. Pippa <u>splashed</u> in the big puddle. [1 mark]
3. Rehan <u>watched</u> the movie. [1 mark]

4. I can get <u>dressed</u> by myself. [1 mark]

5. Dan <u>looked</u> out of the window. [1 mark]

Now try these

The children add the suffix '–ed' to the words 'play' and 'wait', then use them in sentences of their own construction. You may wish to support the children by discussing the task before setting them to work independently or in pairs.

Suggested answers

1. Accept any sentence that includes the word 'played'. [2 marks]

2. Accept any sentence that includes the word 'waited'. [2 marks]

Support, embed & challenge

Support

Use Vocabulary Unit 2B Resource 1: Adding –ed to verbs to provide these children with practice in reading, writing and understanding words that end in the '–ed' suffix but do not need changes made to the root word. Ask the children to read the word sums and write the new words. Use the resource sheet to discuss the spellings, pronunciations and meanings of the words. Extend the task by asking the children to put some of the words into sentences, either orally or written. (**Answers** 1. showed, 2. looked, 3. counted, 4. picked, 5. asked, 6. pressed, 7. answered, 8. cleaned)

Embed

Use Vocabulary Unit 2B Resource 2: Past or future tense? to consolidate the children's understanding that the the suffix '–ed' is used to talk and write about the past. Ask the children to read each sentence and tick boxes to say whether it happened in the past or whether it hasn't happened yet. (**Answers** 1. I jumped into the mud. [It happened in the past.] 2. I will jump into the mud. [It hasn't happened yet.] 3. I finished tidying my bedroom. [It happened in the past.] 4. I will finish tidying my bedroom. [It hasn't happened yet.] 5. I coloured the picture. [It happened in the past.] 6. I am going to colour the picture. [It hasn't happened yet.])

Challenge

Challenge these children to think about the three different sounds represented by the suffix '–ed'. Explain and model that in some words the suffix '–ed' doesn't add another syllable and is pronounced like a 't', as in 'looked', or a 'd', as in 'showed', and in other words the suffix '–ed' is pronounced as 'ed' and adds an extra syllable, as in 'counted'. Ask the children to investigate the words they have been using in the Pupil Book or the resource sheets and to sort them into three lists according to the three sounds.

Homework / Additional activities

Finding –ed

Ask the children to talk to their parents about the suffix '–ed' and notice it in their reading book. You could ask parents to help children find more examples and bring them to school to share with the class.

Collins Connect: Vocabulary Unit 2

Ask the children to complete Vocabulary Unit 2 (See Teach → Year 1 → Vocabulary, Grammar and Punctuation → Vocabulary Unit 2).

Note: the Collins Connect activities could be used with Unit 2A, 2B, 2C and 2D.

Vocabulary Unit 2C: Adding endings to root words (–er)

Overview

English curriculum objectives
- **Suffixes** that can be added to **verbs** [and **adjectives**] where no change is needed in the spelling of root words (e.g. 'helping', 'helped', 'helper')

Treasure House resources
- Vocabulary, Grammar and Punctuation Skills Pupil Book 1, Vocabulary Unit 2C, pages 12–13

- Collins Connect Treasure House Vocabulary, Grammar and Punctuation Year 1, Vocabulary Unit 2
- Photocopiable Vocabulary Unit 2C, Resource 1: Using adjectives to compare, page 73
- Photocopiable Vocabulary Unit 2C, Resource 2: About me, page 74

Additional resources
- Pictures of people with identifiable professions, and objects that perform functions

Introduction

Teaching overview

The suffix '–er' can be added to some verbs to make nouns to name people or things that perform the action of or are concerned with the verb, for example: 'producer', 'chopper', 'washer'. Many nouns formed from verbs by the addition of '–er' are used to name professions. The suffix '–er' can also be added to adjectives to create comparative adjectives. This unit focuses on adding the suffix '–er' without needing to change the spelling of the root word. Use the content of this unit to actively develop children's oral vocabulary as well as their ability to understand and use the grammatical structures, giving particular support to children whose oral language skills are insufficiently developed. When modelling the teaching point, use your voice to show emphasis, intonation, tone, volume and natural speech patterns. This will help beginner learners to bridge the gaps between spoken and written vocabulary, grammar and punctuation.

Introduce the concept

Show pictures of people with identifiable professions, and objects that perform functions, ensuring the names of the professions and the objects are all formed from verbs and the suffix '–er', for example: 'teacher', 'builder', 'cleaner', 'dishwasher', 'hairdryer', 'hanger'. Ask the children what each profession or object is and write the nouns on the board. Ask the children what all the words have in common. Take suggestions and establish that they all end '–er' and

that they are all nouns. Underline one of the root verbs in one of the nouns. Ask the children what sort of word it is and agree that it is a verb. Discuss the action it describes. Repeat the process for some of the other examples. Help the children to see the connection in meaning between the root verbs and the professions or functions that the nouns name. For example, ask: 'What is the noun "teacher" made from?' Agree that it comprises the verb 'teach' and the suffix '–er'. Ask: 'What does a teacher do?' Agree that they teach.

Tell the children that they can also add '–er' to adjectives when they want to compare things. Write the word 'tall' on the board and ensure all the children understand what it means and recognise that it is an adjective. Draw a skyscraper on the board next to the word 'tall'. Say: 'This is a tall building.' Draw a taller skyscraper next to the first. Say: 'This building is taller.' Write the word 'taller' next to the second drawing. Underline the two components in the word, 'tall' and '–er'. Ensure the children can recognise the root adjective and the suffix. Point out that, when '–er' is added to adjectives, they stay as adjectives but the meaning changes so that we can use them to compare things. Provide more examples (with drawings), such as 'small' and 'smaller', 'cold' and 'colder', 'fast' and 'faster', 'high' and 'higher'.

Read and point to the teaching point in the Pupil Book: 'We can change words by adding the ending '–er'. An ending like this is called a suffix. The teacher was reading a story. My brother is louder than me!'

Pupil practice

Get started

The children copy sentences, then find and underline the suffix '–er'. You may wish to support the children by reading each sentence aloud, then pausing while they find and point to the suffix '–er', before asking them to copy the sentences.

Answers

1. *Max is a farmer in the next town.* *[example]*

2. I ran faster along the path than my cat. [1 mark]

3. The sun seems brighter in the afternoon. [1 mark]

4. Every year I grow taller. [1 mark]

5. The kite flew higher into the sky. [1 mark]

Try these

The children copy and correct sentences by adding the suffix '–er' to the underlined words.

Answers

1. *The gardener has green fingers.* *[example]*

2. The nights are getting even colder. [1 mark]

3. I am older than my sister. [1 mark]

4. The duckling was growing ever stronger. [1 mark]

5. Adding sugar makes food taste sweeter than before. [1 mark]

Now try these

The children add the suffix '–er' to the words 'tight' and 'dark', then use them in sentences of their own construction. You may wish to support the children by discussing the task before setting them to work independently or in pairs.

Suggested answers

1. Accept any sentence that includes the word 'tighter'. [2 marks]

2. Accept any sentence that includes the word 'darker'. [2 marks]

Support, embed & challenge

Support

Use Vocabulary Unit 2C Resource 1: Using adjectives to compare to provide these children with practice in using adjectives ending '–er' to compare two things. Model the task using the example sentence, then read the other sentences aloud emphasising the word 'but' to suggest that children should join in and say the remainder of the sentence. Help children to spell the remainder of the sentences as necessary. (**Answers** 1. *Annie's sunflower is tall but Emma's sunflower is taller. [example]* 2. Zain can run fast but Harry can run faster. 3. My lamp is bright but the sun is brighter. 4. The days are cold but the nights are colder. 5. Your grandpa is old but mine is older. 6. A mouse is small but a bee is even smaller.)

Embed

Use Vocabulary Unit 2C Resource 2: About me to encourage the children to use words ending in the suffix '–er' when comparing themselves to others. Ask the children to complete the sentences about themselves. For each sentence, they should choose an adjective from the box and write it in the first gap. Then they should write the name of a person or a thing in the second gap. For the last two sentences, they should think of their own adjectives.

Challenge

Ask these children to think about job titles ending '–er', such as 'farmer', 'teacher', 'gardener', 'painter', 'dog walker', 'banker'. Challenge them to think of three job titles that end '–er' and then write a sentence for each one to describe the job, for example: 'A dog walker takes dogs for walks.' 'A painter paints pictures.' 'A banker works in a bank.'

Homework / Additional activities

Finding –er

Ask the children to talk to their parents about the suffix '–er'. Ask parents to point out words with this ending in the children's home reading books.

Collins Connect: Vocabulary Unit 2

Ask the children to complete Vocabulary Unit 2 (See Teach → Year 1 → Vocabulary, Grammar and Punctuation → Vocabulary Unit 2).

Note: the Collins Connect activities could be used with Unit 2A, 2B, 2C and 2D.

Vocabulary Unit 2D: Adding endings to root words (–est)

Overview

English curriculum objectives

- **Suffixes** that can be added to **verbs** [and **adjectives**] where no change is needed in the spelling of root words (e.g. 'helping', 'helped', 'helper')

Treasure House resources

- Vocabulary, Grammar and Punctuation Skills Pupil Book 1, Vocabulary Unit 2D, pages 14–15

- Collins Connect Treasure House Vocabulary, Grammar and Punctuation Year 1, Vocabulary Unit 2
- Photocopiable Vocabulary Unit 2D, Resource 1: Rosettes, page 75
- Photocopiable Vocabulary Unit 2D, Resource 2: Labels, page 76

Introduction

Teaching overview

This unit builds on the content of the previous unit on comparative adjectives, used to compare two things. This unit focuses on creating superlative adjectives (adjectives used to describe the most or least of a group of things) by adding the suffix '–est' to adjectives where no change is needed in the spelling of the root words. Use the content of this unit to actively develop children's oral vocabulary as well as their ability to understand and use the grammatical structures, giving particular support to children whose oral language skills are insufficiently developed. When modelling the teaching point, use your voice to show emphasis, intonation, tone, volume and natural speech patterns. This will help beginner learners to bridge the gaps between spoken and written vocabulary, grammar and punctuation.

Introduce the concept

Ask the children: 'Who do you think is the fastest runner in the class?' Allow some discussion before

moving on and asking: 'Who do you think is the loudest person in the class?' Again, allow some discussion before moving on. Display the following words on the board: 'fastest', 'loudest'. Discuss the meaning of each word. Then ask the children: 'What do these words have in common?' Establish that they both end in '–est' and are both adjectives. Point out the root adjective in each word. Explain that, if we want to say someone or something is the most or least anything, we need to use an adjective ending '–est'. Model using adjectives ending '–est' in sentences and invite volunteers to do the same, for example: 'I am the oldest person in this classroom.' 'This is the sharpest pencil in my pencil case.'

Read and point to the teaching point in the Pupil Book: 'We can change words by adding the ending '–est'. An ending like this is called a suffix. We travelled on the slowest bus. I am the tallest child in my class.'

Pupil practice

Pupil Book pages 14–15

Get started

The children copy sentences, then find and underline the suffix '–est'. You may wish to support the children by reading each sentence aloud, then pausing while they find and point to the suffix '–est', before asking them to copy the sentences.

Answers

1. *Zak was the fast<u>est</u> boy in the race.* *[example]*
2. Our car is the clean<u>est</u>. [1 mark]
3. Raj is the loud<u>est</u> singer. [1 mark]
4. My pencil is the sharp<u>est</u> in the pot. [1 mark]
5. I am the young<u>est</u> in my family. [1 mark]

Try these

The children copy sentences and add the suffix '–est' to the underlined words.

Answers

1. *I ate the <u>thickest</u> slice of bread.* *[example]*
2. Today is the <u>longest</u> day of the year. [1 mark]
3. I have the <u>softest</u> teddy of them all. [1 mark]
4. I put the book on the <u>lowest</u> shelf. [1 mark]
5. Mum chose the <u>lightest</u> shade of blue. [1 mark]

Now try these

The children add the suffix '–est' to the words 'old' and 'smart', then use them in sentences of their own construction. You may wish to support the children by discussing the task before setting them to work independently or in pairs.

Suggested answers

1. Accept any sentence that includes the word 'oldest'. [2 marks]
2. Accept any sentence that includes the word 'smartest'. [2 marks]

Support, embed & challenge

Support

Use Vocabulary Unit 2D Resource 1: Rosettes to familiarise these children with adjectives ending '–est'. Ask the children to think about who they know that fits the description under each rosette and then write that person's name in the middle.

Embed

Use Vocabulary Unit 2D Resource 2: Labels to provide the children with practice in using words ending '–est'. Ask the children to read through all the words and discuss with a partner (or in a group) what each word means. Then direct the children to look at the images and label each one with an appropriate '–est' word from the box.

Challenge

Challenge these children to write a short story about a mouse called Marvin using the words 'grandest', 'smartest' and 'richest'.

Homework / Additional activities

Family comparisons

Ask the children to talk with their families about words ending in '–est'. Ask them to make a note of who in their family is the tallest, shortest, oldest and youngest.

Collins Connect: Vocabulary Unit 2

Ask the children to complete Vocabulary Unit 2 (See Teach → Year 1 → Vocabulary, Grammar and Punctuation → Vocabulary Unit 2).

Note: the Collins Connect activities could be used with Unit 2A, 2B, 2C and 2D.

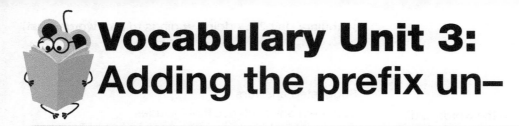

Vocabulary Unit 3:
Adding the prefix un–

Overview

English curriculum objectives
- How the **prefix** un– changes the meaning of **verbs** and **adjectives** [negation, for example, 'unkind', or 'undoing': 'untie the boat']

Treasure House resources
- Vocabulary, Grammar and Punctuation Skills Pupil Book 1, Vocabulary Unit 3, pages 16–17

- Collins Connect Treasure House Vocabulary, Grammar and Punctuation Year 1, Vocabulary Unit 3
- Photocopiable Vocabulary Unit 3, Resource 1: Adding un–, page 77
- Photocopiable Vocabulary Unit 3, Resource 2: Word search, page 78

Introduction

Teaching overview

The prefix 'un–' performs three functions: when combined with adjectives, adverbs, and nouns, it forms words that have the opposite meaning to that of the original root (for example 'untrue', 'unfortunately', 'unhappiness'); when combined with a verb that describes a process, it forms another verb that describes the reverse of that process (for example 'uncover', 'undress'); when combined with a verb's past participle, it forms an adjective that details the process described by the verb as having not happened (for example 'uneaten', 'unseen', 'undiscovered'). This unit focuses on how the prefix 'un–' negates the meanings of verbs and adjectives. Use the content of this unit to actively develop children's oral vocabulary as well as their ability to understand and use the grammatical structures, giving particular support to children whose oral language skills are insufficiently developed. When modelling the teaching point, use your voice to show emphasis, intonation, tone, volume and natural speech patterns. This will help beginner learners to bridge the gaps between spoken and written vocabulary, grammar and punctuation.

Introduce the concept

Ask the children: 'Do you know the word that means the opposite of "fair"?' Allow some discussion and take suggestions. Establish that the opposite of 'fair' is 'unfair'. Write 'fair' and 'unfair' on the board. Next, ask: 'Do you know the word that means the opposite of "lock"?' Again, allow some discussion before establishing that the word is 'unlock'. Write 'lock' and 'unlock' on the board. Ask the children: 'What do these words have in common?' Establish that they both begin with the letters 'un' and that they both mean the opposite of another word. Explain that we can change the meanings of some words to make them mean their opposite by adding the prefix 'un–'.

Read and point to the teaching point in the Pupil Book: 'We can make a word mean its opposite by adding 'un–' to the beginning. Added beginnings like this are called prefixes. Kitty is unfair to her sister Pia. Matt cannot unlock the car to get in.'

Pupil practice

Pupil Book pages 16–17

Get started

The children copy sentences, then find and underline the prefix 'un–'. You may wish to support the children by reading each sentence aloud, then pausing while they find and point to the prefix 'un–', before asking them to copy the sentences.

Answers
1. *Tom cannot <u>un</u>do the box.*   *[example]*
2. Karim will <u>un</u>hook the gate for you.   [1 mark]
3. Meena is <u>un</u>afraid of bugs.   [1 mark]
4. Jenny will <u>un</u>load her bags.   [1 mark]
5. Marc did some <u>un</u>paid jobs.   [1 mark]

Try these

The children copy sentences and add the prefix 'un–' to the underlined words.

Answers
1. *The <u>unlit</u> room was dark.*   *[example]*
2. Eva cannot <u>unstick</u> her teeth from the toffee!   [1 mark]
3. Jayden will <u>unblock</u> the sink for us.   [1 mark]
4. When I go to bed, I <u>undress</u> myself.   [1 mark]
5. Dad is <u>unfit</u> as he likes burgers too much!   [1 mark]

Now try these

The children add the prefix 'un–' to the words 'fair' and 'pack', then use them in sentences of their own construction. You may wish to support the children by discussing the task before setting them to work independently or in pairs.

Suggested answers

1. Accept any sentence that includes the word 'unfair'. [2 marks]

2. Accept any sentence that includes the word 'unpack'. [2 marks]

Support, embed & challenge

Support

Use Vocabulary Unit 3 Resource 1: Adding un– to provide these children with practice in reading, writing and understanding words that begin with the prefix 'un–'. Ask the children to read the word sums and then write the new words. Use the resource sheet to discuss the spellings, pronunciations and meanings of the words. Extend the task by asking the children to put some of the words into sentences, either orally or written. (**Answers** 1. *unfair [example]*, 2. unlock, 3. undo, 4. unhook, 5. unafraid, 6. unload, 7. unpaid, 8. unlit)

Embed

Use Vocabulary Unit 3 Resource 2: Word search to provide the children with practice in reading, recognising and understanding words that begin with the suffix 'un–'. Use the worksheet to discuss the spellings, pronunciations and meanings of the words. Extend the task by asking the children to put some of the words into sentences, either orally or written.

(Answers)

u	n	a	f	r	a	i	d
n	u	n	s	t	i	c	k
d	a	j	d	o	e	u	u
r	u	n	l	i	t	n	n
e	g	k	h	b	f	p	p
s	u	n	f	i	t	a	a
s	c	n	p	l	m	c	i
u	n	b	l	o	c	k	d

Challenge

Challenge these children to think of pairs of words that have opposite meanings (antonym pairs) that do not use the prefix 'un–'. Ask the children to write words that mean the opposite of 'good' ('bad'), 'hot' ('cold'), 'up' ('down'), 'open' ('shut'/'closed') and 'asleep' ('awake'). Challenge them to find more pairs.

Homework / Additional activities

Finding un–

Ask the children to talk to their parents about words that begin with the prefix 'un–'. Ask parents to help their children spot 'un–' words in books they read at home or signs they see when outside.

Collins Connect: Vocabulary Unit 3

Ask the children to complete Vocabulary Unit 3 (See Teach → Year 1 → Vocabulary, Grammar and Punctuation → Vocabulary Unit 3).

Review unit 1: Vocabulary

A. The children copy and correct sentences by adding the suffix '–s' or '–es' to the underlined words.

Answers

1. The <u>boxes</u> are very heavy. [1 mark]

2. I have a pot of <u>grapes</u> with my lunch. [1 mark]

3. My mum bought two <u>bunches</u> of roses. [1 mark]

4. Let's put away all the <u>toys</u>. [1 mark]

B. The children copy and correct sentences by adding the suffix '–ing' or '–ed' to the underlined words.

Answers

1. I <u>washed</u> my hands before I ate. [1 mark]

2. I <u>waited</u> for an hour. [1 mark]

3. We are <u>playing</u> on the slide. [1 mark]

4. Tom was <u>counting</u> his pocket money. [1 mark]

C. The children copy and correct sentences by adding the suffixes '–er' or '–est' to the underlined words.

Answers

5. Jack is <u>taller</u> than Pete but Dan is the <u>tallest</u>. [1 mark]

6. I am <u>older</u> than Iris but Sally is the <u>oldest</u>. [1 mark]

D. The children add the prefix 'un–' to the words 'true' and 'afraid' and the use them in sentences of their own construction.

Suggested answers

7. Accept any sentence that includes the word 'untrue'. [2 marks]

8. Accept any sentence that includes the word 'unafraid'. [2 marks]

Grammar Unit 1A: Building sentences

Overview

English curriculum objectives
- How **words** can combine to make **sentences**

Treasure House resources
- Vocabulary, Grammar and Punctuation Skills Pupil Book 1, Grammar Unit 1A, pages 20–21

- Collins Connect Treasure House Vocabulary, Grammar and Punctuation Year 1, Grammar Unit 1
- Photocopiable Grammar Unit 1A, Resource 1: Making sentences, page 79
- Photocopiable Grammar Unit 1A, Resource 2: Building your own sentences, page 80

Introduction

Teaching overview

A sentence is a group of syntactically related words capable of standing alone to make a statement, ask a question, give a command or exclaim something. Sentences always contain a subject and a verb. This unit introduces children to the concept of making a sentence by putting words in the correct order so that they make sense. Use the content of this unit to actively develop children's oral vocabulary as well as their ability to understand and use the grammatical structures, giving particular support to children whose oral language skills are insufficiently developed. When modelling the teaching point, use your voice to show emphasis, intonation, tone, volume and natural speech patterns. This will help beginner learners to bridge the gaps between spoken and written vocabulary, grammar and punctuation.

Introduce the concept

On the board write: 'the mat sits on The boy'. Read it aloud slowly and clearly and ask the children: 'Is this a sentence? How do we know?' Pause to allow the children to think and then take suggestions. Establish that it might look a bit like a sentence but it doesn't make sense. Ask if the children can help you to rearrange some of the words so that they make sense. Take suggestions and, working with the children, rearrange the words into the sentence: 'The boy sits on the mat.' Point out the capital letter at the beginning and the full stop at the end. Tell the children that every sentence must begin with a capital letter and a full stop. Repeat the activity with the sentence: 'The pond swim on the ducks.'

Read and point to the teaching point in the Pupil Book: 'We can make a sentence when we put words together in the correct order. A sentence needs a capital letter at the start and a full stop at the end.'

Pupil practice

Pupil Book pages 20–21

Get started

The children put words in order to make a sentence. You may wish to support the children by reading the words in aloud, then pausing while they think about which word might start the sentence and so on, before asking them to write the sentences.

Answers

1. *The dog is barking.*	*[example]*
2. The pin drops.	[1 mark]
3. Marvis likes jam.	[1 mark]
4. Tim has the ball.	[1 mark]
5. We look at him.	[1 mark]

Try these

The children copy and complete sentences by selecting and inserting the correct word from a choice of two.

Answers

1. *The fox runs in the woods.*	*[example]*
2. The little bugs dig down.	[1 mark]
3. Sam is in the bath.	[1 mark]
4. The sun is so hot.	[1 mark]
5. I have socks on my feet.	[1 mark]

Now try these

The children write sentences about given topics. You may wish to support children by discussing their sentences before setting them to work independently.

Suggested answers

1. Accept any properly formed sentence about the child's lunch.

> [3 marks: 1 mark for the correct use of a capital letter, 1 mark for the correct use of a full stop and 1 mark for relevant content]

2. Accept any properly formed sentence about the child's family.

> [3 marks: 1 mark for the correct use of a capital letter, 1 mark for the correct use of a full stop and 1 mark for relevant content]

Support, embed & challenge

Support

Use Grammar Unit 1A Resource 1: Making sentences to provide these children with practice in building sentences by putting words in the correct order. Ask the children to cut out the words on the sheet and then help them to read the words and put them in the correct order. You could ask them to stick the sentences in a notebook or on a piece of paper. They could also illustrate the sentences to demonstrate their understanding of the content. (**Answers** The children played at the park. The rabbit dug a deep burrow. The kite flew in the wind.)

Embed

Use Grammar Unit 1A Resource 2: Building your own sentences to give the children the opportunity to explore building their own sentences. Ask the children to cut out all the words. Then ask them to experiment selecting words and placing them in the correct order to make sentences. You could ask the children to copy down some of the sentences they make.

Challenge

Ask these children to think about the order of words in sentence. Challenge them to write muddled up sentences for a partner to unscramble.

Homework / Additional activities

Orderly manner

Ask the children to explain to their parents about why the order of words in a sentence matters.

Collins Connect: Grammar Unit 1

Ask the children to complete Grammar Unit 1 (See Teach → Year 1 → Vocabulary, Grammar and Punctuation → Grammar Unit 1).

Note: the Collins Connect activities could be used with Unit 1A or 1B.

Grammar Unit 1B: Building more sentences

Overview

English curriculum objectives
- How **words** can combine to make **sentences**

Treasure House resources
- Vocabulary, Grammar and Punctuation Skills Pupil Book 1, Grammar Unit 1B, pages 22–23

- Collins Connect Treasure House Vocabulary, Grammar and Punctuation Year 1, Grammar Unit 1
- Photocopiable Grammar Unit 1B, Resource 1: Is it a sentence? page 81
- Photocopiable Grammar Unit 1B, Resource 2: Finishing sentences, page 82

Introduction

Teaching overview

This unit builds on the previous unit to provide further practice in building sentences by putting words in the correct order so that they make sense. Use the content of this unit to actively develop children's oral vocabulary as well as their ability to understand and use the grammatical structures, giving particular support to children whose oral language skills are insufficiently developed. When modelling the teaching point, use your voice to show emphasis, intonation, tone, volume and natural speech patterns. This will help beginner learners to bridge the gaps between spoken and written vocabulary, grammar and punctuation.

Introduce the concept

On the board, write: 'Tim bike likes his to ride'. Read it aloud slowly and clearly and ask the children: 'Is this a sentence? How do we know?' Pause to allow the children to think and then take suggestions. Establish that it looks a bit like a sentence but it doesn't make sense. Ask the children to help you to rearrange the words to make a sentence. Take suggestions and, with the children's support, rearrange the words to read 'Tim likes to ride his bike.' Point out the capital letter at the beginning and the full stop at the end. Repeat the activity with the sentence 'The rabbits field in the hop.' Read and point to the teaching point in the Pupil Book: 'Remember, we can make a sentence when we put words together in the correct order. A sentence needs a capital letter at the start and a full stop at the end.'

Pupil practice

Pupil Book pages 22–23

Get started

The children put words in order to make a sentence. You may wish to support the children by reading the words aloud, then pausing while they think about which word might start the sentence and so on, before asking them to write the sentences.

Answers

1. *The cat is purring.*   *[example]*
2. The rain falls.   [1 mark]
3. Samira likes cake.   [1 mark]
4. Faisal has the book.   [1 mark]
5. We all played a game.   [1 mark]

Try these

The children copy and complete sentences by selecting and inserting the correct word from a choice of two.

Answers

1. *The deer hides in the grass.*   *[example]*
2. The little bird builds a nest.   [1 mark]

3. Maria is in the garden.   [1 mark]
4. The stars sparkle in the night sky.   [1 mark]
5. I have shoes on my feet.   [1 mark]

Now try these

The children write sentences about given topics. You may wish to support children by discussing their sentences before setting them to work independently.

Suggested answers

1. Accept any properly formed sentence about the student's school.
   [3 marks: 1 mark for the correct use of a capital letter, 1 mark for the correct use of a full stop and 1 mark for relevant content]

2. Accept any properly formed sentence about the student's favourite toy.
   [3 marks: 1 mark for the correct use of a capital letter, 1 mark for the correct use of a full stop and 1 mark for relevant content]

Support, embed & challenge

Subject sentences

Use Grammar Unit 1B Resource 1: Is it a sentence? to provide these children with practice in reading and recognising when sentences make sense because the words are in the correct order. Ask the children to read the sentences then tick 'yes' if they make sense and 'no' if they do not make sense. (**Answers** 1. I hair my brushed. [no] 2. We had soup for lunch. [yes] 3. Pen my is blue. [no] 4. Today sunny is a day. [no] 5. I packed my bag. [yes] 6. We had yes and. [no] 7. You are my best friend. [yes] 8. Like I fish chips and. [no])

Embed

Use Grammar Unit 1B Resource 2: Finishing sentences to give the children the opportunity to write their own sentences that make sense. Read the sentence starters aloud and ask the children to complete them. You may wish to provide additional support in the form of a word bank on the board, including, for example: 'woke up', 'got dressed' 'had breakfast', 'talked to my friends', 'saw a dog', 'walked', 'football', 'hide and seek', 'make believe', 'lunch box', 'school dinner', 'pasta', 'sandwiches'.

Challenge

Challenge these children to list the main characteristics of a sentence. (A complete sentence communicates a complete thought, is made up of a subject and a verb, starts with a capital letter and has end punctuation.) Invite them to present their lists to the other children.

Homework / Additional activities

Subject sentences

Ask the children to write complete sentences on a subject of their choice.

Collins Connect: Grammar Unit 1

Ask the children to complete Grammar Unit 1 (See Teach → Year 1 → Vocabulary, Grammar and Punctuation → Unit 1).

Note: the Collins Connect activities could be used with Unit 1A or 1B.

Grammar Unit 2A:
Building sentences using 'and'

Overview

English curriculum objectives
- Joining **words** and joining **clauses** using 'and'

Treasure House resources
- Vocabulary, Grammar and Punctuation Skills Pupil Book 1, Grammar Unit 2A, pages 24–25
- Collins Connect Treasure House Vocabulary, Grammar and Punctuation Year 1, Grammar Unit 2

- Photocopiable Grammar Unit 2A, Resource 1: Joining sentences, page 83
- Photocopiable Grammar Unit 2A, Resource 2: Building sentences using 'and', page 84

Additional resources
- Texts containing sentences that use 'and'

Introduction

Teaching overview
This unit introduces the children to the concept of joining words and joining clauses using 'and'. The word 'and' is a coordinating conjunction. Coordinating conjunctions connect words, phrases, clauses and sentences of equal syntactic importance. Use the content of this unit to actively develop children's oral vocabulary as well as their ability to understand and use the grammatical structures, giving particular support to children whose oral language skills are insufficiently developed. When modelling the teaching point, use your voice to show emphasis, intonation, tone, volume and natural speech patterns. This will help beginner learners to bridge the gaps between spoken and written vocabulary, grammar and punctuation.

Introduce the concept
On the board, write: 'She likes books. She likes maps.' Read both sentences aloud slowly and clearly and ask the children: 'Are these sentences? How do we know?' Pause to allow children to think and then take suggestions. Establish that both groups of words make sense and start with a capital letter and end with a full stop, therefore they are sentences. Tell the children that you are going to show them how they can make their sentences more interesting to read and help them to sound more natural. Write the sentence 'She likes books and she likes maps.' Read the whole sentence aloud and ask the children to comment on what you have changed. Establish that you added the word 'and' to join the sentences together. Repeat the activity with the sentence: 'The sun is up and it is hot.'

Read and point to the teaching point in the Pupil Book: 'We can join two short sentences together with the linking word 'and'. This makes two sentences into one longer sentence.'

Pupil practice

Pupil Book pages 24–25

Get started
The children copy sentences and underline the word 'and'. You may wish to support the children by reading the sentences, then pausing while they find and point to the word 'and', before asking them to write the sentences.

Answers
1. *She brushes her hair <u>and</u> she brushes her teeth.* [example]
2. I can hop <u>and</u> you can jump. [1 mark]
3. I like bats <u>and</u> he likes hats. [1 mark]
4. I can swim <u>and</u> we can sail. [1 mark]
5. Jaz will sing <u>and</u> he will shout. [1 mark]

Try these
The children copy and complete sentences by inserting the word 'and'.

1. *I can stomp <u>and</u> you can stamp.* [example]
2. She can hear bells <u>and</u> she can hear horns. [1 mark]
3. I go to you <u>and</u> you come to me. [1 mark]
4. It is raining <u>and</u> we are getting wet. [1 mark]
5. It is winter <u>and</u> you have a chill. [1 mark]

Now try these

The children put words in the correct order to make sentences. You may wish to support children by discussing their sentences before setting them to work independently.

1. We see bees and we see flowers. /
   We see flowers and we see bees. [1 mark]

2. He likes swinging and she likes running. /
   He likes running and she likes swinging. [1 mark]

Support, embed & challenge

Support

Use Grammar Unit 2A Resource 1: Joining sentences to help the children to understand how to join two sentences that are on a similar topic using the word 'and'. Read the sentence parts aloud to the children and model how to complete the resource sheet. Then ask the children to draw lines to join the sentence parts together, looking for the topics that match. (**Answers** I like yellow and I like red. I count to ten and you count to twenty. My hair is long and your hair is short. It is a hot day and I would like an ice-cream. I like to play cars and I like to play trains. I like to drink milk and I like to drink juice.)

Embed

Use Grammar Unit 2A Resource 2: Building sentences using and to help the children to practise building sentences that use 'and' by putting words in the correct order. Ask the children to cut out the words, and then support them to read the words and put them in the correct order. You could ask the children to stick the sentences in a notebook or on a piece of paper. They could also illustrate the sentences to show their understanding of the content. (**Answers** It is snowing and we are cold. I like running and I like hopping. / I like hopping and I like running.)

Challenge

Challenge these children to go on a sentence hunt, looking for sentences that use the word 'and'. Tell them to look through their reading book, or a selection of classroom books, and note down examples of sentences they find that use 'and'.

Homework / Additional activities

My family and me

Ask the children to talk to their parents about sentences that contain the linking word 'and'. Ask parents to help their child spot sentences that use 'and' in books they read at home or signs they see when outside.

Collins Connect: Grammar Unit 2

Ask the children to complete Grammar Unit 2 (See Teach → Vocabulary, Grammar and Punctuation → Year 1 → Grammar Unit 2).

Note: the Collins Connect activities could be used with Unit 2A or 2B.

Grammar Unit 2B: Building more sentences using 'and'

Overview

English curriculum objectives
- Joining **words** and joining **clauses** using 'and'

Treasure House resources
- Vocabulary, Grammar and Punctuation Skills Pupil Book 1, Grammar Unit 2B, pages 26–27
- Collins Connect Treasure House Vocabulary, Grammar and Punctuation Year 1, Grammar Unit 2

- Photocopiable Grammar Unit 2B, Resource 1: Is it a sentence? page 85
- Photocopiable Grammar Unit 2B, Resource 2: Completing sentences using 'but', page 86

Additional resources
- Texts containing sentences with coordinating conjunctions

Introduction

Teaching overview

This unit builds on the previous unit, providing further practice joining words and joining clauses using 'and'. The word 'and' is a coordinating conjunction. Coordinating conjunctions connect words, phrases, clauses and sentences of equal syntactic importance. The children will also be introduced to the coordinating conjunction 'but', which is used to connect words, phrases, clauses and sentences of equal syntactic importance that express contrasting ideas or facts. Use the content of this unit to actively develop children's oral vocabulary as well as their ability to understand and use the grammatical structures, giving particular support to children whose oral language skills are insufficiently developed. When modelling the teaching point, use your voice to show emphasis, intonation, tone, volume and natural speech patterns. This will help beginner learners to bridge the gaps between spoken and written vocabulary, grammar and punctuation.

Introduce the concept

On the board, write: 'She likes reading. She likes drawing.' Read both sentences aloud slowly and clearly and ask: 'Are these sentences? How do we know?' Pause to allow the children to think and then take suggestions. Establish that both groups of words make sense and start with a capital letter and end with a full stop, therefore they are sentences. Tell the children that you are going to show them how they can make their sentences more interesting to read and help them to sound more natural. Write 'She likes reading and she likes drawing.' Read the whole sentence aloud and ask the children to comment on what you have changed. Establish that you added the word 'and' to join the sentences together. Repeat the activity with the sentence 'The wind is blowing and it is cold.'

Read and point to the teaching point in the Pupil Book: 'Remember, we can join two short sentences together with the linking word 'and'. This makes two sentences into one longer sentence.'

Pupil practice

Pupil Book pages 26–27

Get started

The children copy sentences and underline the word 'and'. You may wish to support the children by reading the sentences, then pausing while they find and point to the word 'and', before asking them to write the sentences.

Answers
1. *She put on her coat <u>and</u> she put on her shoes.*   *[example]*
2. I can throw <u>and</u> you can catch.   [1 mark]
3. I like apples <u>and</u> he likes pears.   [1 mark]
4. I will count <u>and</u> you can hide.   [1 mark]
5. Mum will cook <u>and</u> we will watch.   [1 mark]

Try these

The children copy and complete sentences by inserting the word 'and'.

Answers
1. *I can shout <u>and</u> you can whisper.*   *[example]*
2. She hears drums <u>and</u> she hears a tambourine.   [1 mark]
3. I call to you <u>and</u> you answer me.   [1 mark]
4. We go swimming <u>and</u> we have fun.   [1 mark]
5. It is summer <u>and</u> we are hot.   [1 mark]

Now try these

The children put words in the correct order to make sentences. You may wish to support children by discussing their sentences before setting them to work independently.

Answers

1. We see birds and we see planes. /
   We see planes and we see birds.   [1 mark]
2. He likes painting and she likes counting. /
   He likes counting and she likes painting.   [1 mark]

Support, embed & challenge

Support

Use Grammar Unit 2B Resource 1: Is it a sentence? to encourage these children to consider whether sentences make sense. Read the sentences with the children and ask them to think about whether they sound right, whether there are any words missing, whether there is a capital letter at the start and whether there is a full stop at the end. Ask the children to tick 'yes' or 'no' to indicate whether each line is a sentence or not. (**Answers** 1. I brush my hair I brush my teeth [no] 2. We had salad and we had chips. [yes] 3. I have a red pen and I have a pink pen. [yes] 4. I am going to shop I am going to park [no] 5. I put on my coat and I put on my shoes. [yes] 6. The pirates read the map and found the treasure. [yes] 7. Sam tidied his room did his homework. [no] 8. We are chatting listening to music. [no])

Embed

Use Grammar Unit 2B Resource 2: Completing sentences using 'but' to embed and extend the children's understanding of making longer and more interesting sentences by introducing 'but' as a linking word. Explain that the word 'but' acts in a similar way to 'and', as a linking word to join sentences, but that it has a different meaning. 'And' is used to add something similar; 'but' is used to add something different (contrasting). Read the sentences and ask children to write the word 'but' in the gaps. Then encourage the children to read the completed sentences and consider what they mean. (**Answers** 1. I am hot but I don't want to take off my coat. 2. I like playing cars but I like playing with blocks more. 3. I have a friend called Bob but I also have a friend called Peter. 4. I am good at counting but I am not good at adding. 5. I like rabbits but I do not like cats.)

Challenge

Challenge these children to go on a sentence hunt looking for sentences that use the coordinating conjunctions 'and', 'but' and 'or'. Tell them to look through their reading book or a selection of classroom books and note down examples of sentences they find that use these conjunctions.

Homework / Additional activities

Where are the buts?

Ask the children to talk to their parents about sentences that contain the linking word 'but'. Ask parents to help their child spot sentences that use 'but' in books they read at home or signs they see when outside.

Collins Connect: Grammar Unit 2

Ask the children to complete Grammar Unit 2 (See Teach → Year 1 → Vocabulary, Grammar and Punctuation → Grammar Unit 2).

Note: the Collins Connect activities could be used with Unit 2A or 2B.

Review unit 2: Grammar

Pupil Book pages 28–29

A. The children put words in the correct order to make a sentence.

Answers

1. The cat is asleep. [1 mark]
2. I like to splash in puddles. [1 mark]
3. We climbed the tree. [1 mark]
4. My jumper is red. [1 mark]

B. The children copy and complete each sentence by selecting the correct word from a choice of two. Remind them that the sentence should make sense.

Answers

1. The ice cubes were melting. [1 mark]
2. Anna is riding her bike. [1 mark]
3. We made a snowman. [1 mark]
4. The bee landed on the flower. [1 mark]

C. The children write a sentence about today.

Suggested answer

1. Accept any properly formed sentence about the given topic that has a capital letter at the start and a full stop at the end.

[3 marks: 1 mark for the correct use of a capital letter, 1 mark for the correct use of a full stop and 1 mark for relevant content]

D. The children use the word 'and' to join each pair of sentences together.

Answers

1. I like fish and I like chips. [1 mark]
2. I will throw and you can catch. [1 mark]
3. Birds build nests and they eat bugs. [1 mark]
4. Ben plays with cars and Lisa draws a picture. [1 mark]

E. The children put words in the correct order to make sentences.

Answers

1. We picked strawberries and we made jam. / We made jam and we picked strawberries. [1 mark]
2. I have a pencil and I have a sharpener. / I have a sharpener and I have a pencil. [1 mark]

Punctuation Unit 1:
Leaving spaces between words

Overview

English curriculum objectives
- Separation of **words** with spaces

Treasure House resources
- Vocabulary, Grammar and Punctuation Skills Pupil Book 1, Punctuation Unit 1, pages 30–31

- Photocopiable Punctuation Unit 1, Resource 1: Word snakes, page 87
- Photocopiable Punctuation Unit 1, Resource 2: Spaces between words, page 88

Introduction

Teaching overview

This unit introduces children to the concept that a sentence must have spaces between the words for it to be readable. Use the content of this unit to actively develop children's oral vocabulary as well as their ability to understand and use the grammatical structures, giving particular support to children whose oral language skills are insufficiently developed. When modelling the teaching point, use your voice to show emphasis, intonation, tone, volume and natural speech patterns. This will help beginner learners to bridge the gaps between spoken and written vocabulary, grammar and punctuation.

Introduce the concept

On the board, write: 'Asentenceishardtoreadwithnospaces.' Ask the

children whether they can read what you have written. Pause to allow the children to try and then take suggestions. Establish that it is a string of squashed-up words and, because there are no spaces between the words, it is very hard to read. Tell the children that you are going to work together to try to read the words and see what the sentence is supposed to say. Slowly sound out the words with emphasis and intonation to enable the children to hear the individual words. As you work through the letter string together, write the words on the board, this time with spaces: 'A sentence is hard to read with no spaces.'

Read and point to the teaching point in the Pupil Book: 'A sentence is a group of words that makes sense. The words must be in the correct order and there must be spaces between the words.'

Pupil practice

Pupil Book pages 30–31

Get started

The children copy and correct sentences by adding spaces between the words. You may wish to support the children by modelling how to read the sounds in each sentence aloud very slowly, then pausing while they discern the individual words, before asking them to copy the sentences.

Answers

1. *The horse runs fast.*   *[example]*
2. The sky is blue.   [1 mark]
3. I like apples.   [1 mark]
4. The boy kicked the football. [1 mark]
5. The sun is shining.   [1 mark]

Try these

The children copy and correct sentences by putting the words in the correct order and adding spaces between the words.

Answers

1. *The film was funny.*   *[example]*
2. My cat likes milk.   [1 mark]
3. The grass is green.   [1 mark]
4. Spiders have eight legs.   [1 mark]
5. I won the race.   [1 mark]

Now try these

The children add spaces between words in longer sentences. You may wish to support children by reading the words in the sentences together before setting them to work independently.

Answers

1. The elephants marched down to the river to get a drink.   [1 mark]
2. The children wrote stories about the lost parrot.   [1 mark]

Support, embed & challenge

Support

Use Punctuation Unit 1 Resource 1: Word snakes to emphasise to these children how difficult it is to read words when there are no spaces between them. Searching for words within word snakes provides a fun way to make the teaching point as well as providing practice in focusing on details. Ask the children to look carefully through the word snakes and circle the words they find. (**Answers** 1. one, two, three, four, five; 2. red, yellow, blue, green, orange; 3. dog, cat, mouse, bird, horse; 4. trains, cars, blocks, bikes, balls)

Embed

Use Punctuation Unit 1 Resource 2: Spaces between words to provide the children with practice in writing sentences with appropriately sized spaces between the words. On the board, model the difference between spaces that are too big and spaces that are too small. Tell the children that the best way to improve the size of their spaces is to practise. Ask the children to separate the words in the sentences and rewrite them with spaces. (**Answers** 1. The sheep were grazing. 2. The hens were clucking. 3. The dog was barking. 4. The cows were eating. 5. The farmer was digging.)

Challenge

Challenge these children to design a poster that reminds writers to leave spaces between the words in sentences.

Homework / Additional activities

Spacing out

Ask the children to talk to their parents about spaces between words in sentences. Suggest that children look at their parents' handwriting or ask their parents to write a sentence for them so they can see the spaces between the words.

Punctuation Unit 2: Using a capital letter and a full stop

Overview

English curriculum objectives
- Introduction to capital letters, full stops, question marks and exclamation marks to demarcate **sentences**

Treasure House resources
- Vocabulary, Grammar and Punctuation Skills Pupil Book 1, Punctuation Unit 2, pages 32–33
- Photocopiable Punctuation Unit 2, Resource 1: Matching letters, page 89
- Photocopiable Punctuation Unit 2, Resource 2: Writing capital letters, page 90

Introduction

Teaching overview

When written, a sentence begins with a capital letter and concludes with a full stop, question mark or exclamation mark, according to the sentence type. This unit introduces children to the concept that a sentence must start with a capital letter and that most will end with a full stop. Use the content of this unit to actively develop children's oral vocabulary as well as their ability to understand and use the grammatical structures, giving particular support to children whose oral language skills are insufficiently developed. When modelling the teaching point, use your voice to show emphasis, intonation, tone, volume and natural speech patterns. This will help beginner learners to bridge the gaps between spoken and written vocabulary, grammar and punctuation.

Introduce the concept

On the board, write: 'we ate curry for dinner'. Do not include a capital letter at the start or a full stop at the end. Ask the children: 'Have I written a sentence? How do you know?' Pause to allow children to think and then take suggestions. Establish that, although it may look like a sentence because it is a group of words that makes sense, it neither starts with a capital letter nor ends in a full stop. Ask a volunteer to come to the board to correct your sentence by adding a capital letter and a full stop. Repeat the process with the sentence 'Molly read a book about sharks.'

Read and point to the teaching point in the Pupil Book: 'A sentence is a group of words that makes sense. Every sentence should begin with a capital letter. Most sentences end in a full stop.'

Pupil practice

Pupil Book pages 32–33

Get started

The children copy sentences, find and underline the capital letters and then draw rings around the full stops. You may wish to support the children by reading each sentence aloud, then pausing while they find and point to the capital letters and full stops, before asking them to copy the sentences.

Answers

1. *The farmer has ten cows.*　　　　　*[example]*
2. *I love strawberry ice cream.*　　　[2 marks]
3. *The children were sad.*　　　　　　[2 marks]
4. *We need to tidy up.*　　　　　　　[2 marks]
5. *There are wild ponies in the forest.*　[2 marks]

Try these

The children copy and correct sentences by adding capital letters and full stops.

Answers

1. *We have eaten all the cherries.*　　*[example]*

2. The children played on the swings.　[2 marks]
3. The parrot flew over the rooftops.　[2 marks]
4. We are going on holiday.　　　　　[2 marks]
5. My jumper is red.　　　　　　　　[2 marks]

Now try these

The children write sentences on given topics. You may wish to support the children by discussing their sentences before setting them to work independently.

Suggested answers

1. Accept any properly formed sentence about the child's favourite game.
   [3 marks: 1 mark for the correct use of a capital letter, 1 mark for the correct use of a full stop and 1 mark for relevant content]

2. Accept any properly formed sentence about the child's favourite foods
   [3 marks: 1 mark for the correct use of a capital letter, 1 mark for the correct use of a full stop and 1 mark for relevant content]

Support, embed & challenge

Support

Use Punctuation Unit 2 Resource 1: Matching letters to provide these children with practice in recognising the capital formation of the letters of the alphabet and matching them to their lower-case equivalent. Ask the children to draw lines to match the upper- and lower-case letters. To give these children further support, you could recite the alphabet song and ask the children to practise writing the capital letters by copying those on the resource sheet. (**Answers** a–A, b–B, c–C, d–D, e–E, f–F, g–G, h–H, i–I, j–J, k–K, l–L, m–M, n–N, o–O, p–P, q–Q, r–R, s–S, t–T, u–U, v–V, w–W, x–X, y–Y, z–Z)

Embed

Use Punctuation Unit 2 Resource 2: Writing capital letters to provide the children with practice in recalling and writing the capital formation of the letters of the alphabet. Ask the children to write the correct capital letter next to each lower-case letter. You could also recite the alphabet song and ask the children to practise formation of the letters on the sheet by copying. (**Answers** a–A, b–B, c–C, d–D, e–E, f–F, g–G, h–H, i–I, j–J, k–K, l–L, m–M, n–N, o–O, p–P, q–Q, r–R, s–S, t–T, u–U, v–V, w–W, x–X, y–Y, z–Z)

Challenge

Challenge these children to find all the capital letters of the alphabet that are simply bigger versions of their lower-case counterparts ('C' and 'c', 'O' and 'o', 'V' and 'v', 'S' and 's', 'X' and 'x', 'Z' and 'z'). You could make this into a competition by organising the children into pairs and seeing who can find all the letters first.

Homework / Additional activities

Letters and full stops

Ask the children to talk their parents about capital letters and full stops. Ask parents to point out capital letters and full stops to their children when reading at home.

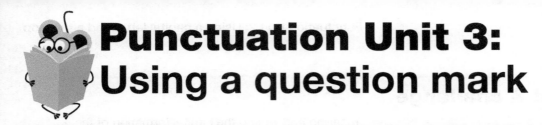

Punctuation Unit 3: Using a question mark

Overview

English curriculum objectives
- Introduction to capital letters, full stops, question marks and exclamation marks to demarcate **sentences**

Treasure House resources
- Vocabulary, Grammar and Punctuation Skills Pupil Book 1, Punctuation Unit 3, pages 34–35
- Photocopiable Punctuation Unit 3, Resource 1: Adding question marks, page 91
- Photocopiable Punctuation Unit 3, Resource 2: Matching questions and answers, page 92

Introduction

Teaching overview

When written, a sentence begins with a capital letter and concludes with a full stop, question mark or exclamation mark, according to the sentence type. This unit introduces children to the concept that a question is a type of sentence that uses a question mark instead of a full stop. Use the content of this unit to actively develop children's oral vocabulary as well as their ability to understand and use the grammatical structures, giving particular support to children whose oral language skills are insufficiently developed. When modelling the teaching point, use your voice to show emphasis, intonation, tone, volume and natural speech patterns. This will help beginner learners to bridge the gaps between spoken and written vocabulary, grammar and punctuation.

Introduce the concept

Ask the children a question, for example: 'What time is it?' 'How did you travel to school today?' 'Who likes the colour yellow?' Write the questions on the board and allow the children to give some answers. Ask:

'What type of sentence is this?' Pause to allow the children to think and then take suggestions. Establish that this type of sentence is called a question. Point to the question mark and ask the children to tell you what it is. Establish that it is a question mark and that its job is to tell the reader that this sentence is a question. On the board, slowly and clearly demonstrate how to draw a question mark. Highlight that a question only has a question mark and does not need a full stop as well. Point out that question sentences still start with a capital letter. Ask the children if they have any questions to ask you, for example: 'Why is the sky blue?' 'Why is the Earth round?' 'Where do polar bears live?' Take their ideas and write them on the board, pointing out and underlining the capital letters and question marks. When they have gained confidence, invite children to underline the capital letters and question marks for you.

Read and point to the teaching point in the Pupil Book: 'A question is a type of sentence. We ask questions to find things out. Questions need a question mark at the end instead of a full stop.'

Pupil practice

Pupil Book pages 34–35

Get started

The children copy sentences, then find and underline the question marks. You may wish to support the children by reading each sentence aloud, then pausing while they find and point to the question mark, before asking them to copy the sentences.

Answers
1. *How many pens are in the pot?* [example]
2. What is your name? [1 mark]
3. How old are you? [1 mark]
4. Do you have any brothers or sisters? [1 mark]
5. What colour are your socks? [1 mark]

Try these

The children copy and correct sentences by adding capital letters and question marks.

Answers
1. *What is your favourite book?* [example]
2. Did you bring a coat with you today? [2 marks]
3. What is your favourite food? [2 marks]
4. Who is your best friend? [2 marks]
5. When is your birthday? [2 marks]

Now try these

The children complete one or both of the tasks: working with a friend to read and answer all of the questions on the page and/or write two questions to ask the teacher. Children could complete the first task orally or by writing their answers.

Suggested answers

1. Accept any answers that are relevant to the questions being asked.   [2 marks]

2. Accept any questions that are appropriate to ask the teacher.

[6 marks: 1 mark per correct use of a capital letter, 1 mark per correct use of a question mark and 1 mark per question sentence]

Support, embed & challenge

Support

Use Punctuation Unit 3 Resource 1: Adding question marks to help these children to recognise questions. Read the sentences with the children and ask if they think each one is a question or not. Discuss why they think it might or might not be a question. Discuss the use of 'question words' such as 'what', 'where', 'when', 'why', 'how' and 'who'. You could also model and demonstrate how the intonation in your voice changes when you ask a question. Ask the children to add the question marks or full stops to the ends of the sentences. (**Answers** 1. Have you been busy today? 2. I am tired. 3. Can you hop on one foot? 4. Are you feeling happy? 5. I need a drink. 6. What day is it? 7. I like reading. 8. Do you like reading?)

Embed

Use Punctuation Unit 3 Resource 2: Matching questions and answers to provide the children with practice reading, recognising and answering questions appropriately. Model reading the first question and show how to read through the different answers until you find the one that matches. Help the children to read the other questions, if necessary, and ask them to draw lines to match them to the answers. (**Answers** 1. What colour is a carrot? c. orange; 2. What time is it? d. It is two o'clock. 3. How old are you? a. I am six years old. 4. What is your favourite food? e. I love pasta. 5. What day is it tomorrow? f. Thursday; 6. What is your favourite toy? b. my teddy)

Challenge

Challenge these children to think of questions they could write for the following answers: 'I like salt and vinegar crisps.' 'It is the colour green.' 'I go to bed at 7pm.'

Homework / Additional activities

Asking questions

Ask the children to talk to their parents about questions and question marks. Ask parents to help their children write a list of questions they could ask their favourite celebrity or fictional character.

Punctuation Unit 4:
Using an exclamation mark

Overview

English curriculum objectives

- Introduction to capital letters, full stops, question marks and exclamation marks to demarcate **sentences**

Treasure House resources

- Vocabulary, Grammar and Punctuation Skills Pupil Book 1, Punctuation Unit 4, pages 36–37

- Photocopiable Punctuation Unit 4, Resource 1: Adding exclamation marks and question marks, page 93
- Photocopiable Punctuation Unit 4, Resource 2: Exclamations, page 94

Additional resources

- Images of emotional characters with speech bubbles displaying sentences that end in exclamation marks

Introduction

Teaching overview

When written, a sentence begins with a capital letter and concludes with a full stop, question mark or exclamation mark, according to the sentence type. This unit introduces children to the concept that an exclamation is a type of sentence that should be said with emphasis and emotion and uses an exclamation mark instead of a full stop. Use the content of this unit to actively develop children's oral vocabulary as well as their ability to understand and use the grammatical structures, giving particular support to children whose oral language skills are insufficiently developed. When modelling the teaching point, use your voice to show emphasis, intonation, tone, volume and natural speech patterns. This will help beginner learners to bridge the gaps between spoken and written vocabulary, grammar and punctuation.

Introduce the concept

Show the children images of emotional characters with speech bubbles displaying sentences that end in exclamation marks. (The images could be from cartoons and comic strips, or you could collect images of emotional characters and add the speech bubbles yourself.) Read through the exclamatory sentences in the speech bubbles. Discuss the emotions displayed by the characters and ask the children in what manner they think the sentences

should be read. Invite the children to demonstrate how they think the sentences should sound. Point out the exclamation mark at the end of each sentence.

On the board, write: 'I can't believe it!' Ask: 'Have I written a sentence?' Pause to allow the children to think and then take suggestions. Establish that this is a type of sentence called an exclamation. Ask the children if they can tell you what an exclamation is or give you any further examples, reminding the children of the sentences they read in the speech bubbles. Clarify that an exclamation is a type of sentence that should be said with emphasis and emotion. Point to the exclamation mark and ask them to tell you what it is. Establish that it is called an exclamation mark and its job is to tell the reader that this sentence is an exclamation and should be read with some surprise, shock or sense of urgency. On the board, demonstrate slowly and clearly how to draw an exclamation mark. Highlight that an exclamation sentence only needs an exclamation mark; it does not need a full stop as well. Point out that the exclamation sentence starts with a capital letter, just the same as every other sentence.

Read and point to the teaching point in the Pupil Book: 'An exclamation is a type of sentence. We make exclamations when we are surprised or feel strongly about something. We need an exclamation mark at the end instead of a full stop.'

Pupil practice

Pupil Book pages 36–37

Get started

The children copy sentences, then find and underline the exclamation marks. You may wish to support the children by reading each sentence aloud, then pausing while they find and point to the exclamation mark, before asking them to copy the sentences.

Answers

1. *Come here quickly!* [example]
2. You are covered in mud! [1 mark]
3. We've found the treasure! [1 mark]
4. What an amazing picture! [1 mark]
5. Help, I'm stuck! [1 mark]

Try these

The children copy and correct the sentences by adding capital letters and exclamation marks.

Answers

1. *The house burned down!*   *[example]*

2. The rain is shocking!   [2 marks]

3. I saw an alien!   [2 marks]

4. We won the competition!   [2 marks]

5. I have had enough of this mess!   [2 marks]

Now try these

The children construct two exclamation sentences. You may wish to support the children by discussing their sentences before setting them to work independently.

Suggested answers

1. Accept any properly formed and punctuated sentences that show an attempt to display shock.

[6 marks: 1 mark per correct use of a capital letter, 1 mark per correct use of an exclamation mark and 1 mark each for relevant content]

2. Accept any properly formed sentences that have capital letters at the start and exclamation marks at the end.

[6 marks: 1 mark per correct use of a capital letter, 1 mark per correct use of an exclamation mark and 1 mark each for relevant content]

Support, embed & challenge

Support

Use Punctuation Unit 4 Resource 1: Adding exclamation marks and question marks to help these children learn to recognise exclamations and to practise recognising questions. Read the sentences with the children and ask if they think each one is an exclamation or a question. For each sentence, discuss why they think it is an exclamation or a question. Demonstrate how the intonation in your voice changes when you read one or the other. Ask the children to add the exclamation marks or question marks to the ends of the sentences. (**Answers** 1. How dreadful! 2. Is it three o'clock yet? 3. What a terrible noise! 4. How very embarrassing! 5. What would you like to drink? 6. Are we nearly there yet?)

Embed

Use Punctuation Unit 4 Resource 2: Exclamations to enable the children to practise reading, recognising

and understanding the intonation required for exclamations. Read the exclamations together and discuss what they mean and how they should be read. Ask the children to draw lines to match the exclamation sentences to the pictures. Ask the children to repeat the intonation you use to read the exclamations. (**Answers** 1. That's impossible! – b. 2. I'm covered in mud! – e. 3. We found the treasure! – d. 4. Help, I'm stuck! – a. 5. The house burned down! c.)

Challenge

Challenge these children to draw cartoons. Ask them to draw a picture of an emotional character with a speech bubble to show what the character is saying. Encourage the children to think about why the character is emotional. Tell them to write a full sentence in the speech bubble and to punctuate the exclamation sentence correctly.

Homework / Additional activities

Exclamations!

Ask the children to talk to their parents about exclamations and exclamation marks. Ask parents to help their children read exclamations with intonation during reading they do at home.

Punctuation Unit 5:
Using a capital letter for names of people

Overview

English curriculum objectives
* Using a capital letter for names of people, places, the days of the week and the personal pronoun 'I'

Treasure House resources
* Vocabulary, Grammar and Punctuation Skills Pupil Book 1, Punctuation Unit 5, pages 38–39

* Collins Connect Treasure House Vocabulary, Grammar and Punctuation Year 1, Punctuation Unit 2
* Photocopiable Punctuation Unit 5, Resource 1: Capital letters for people's names, page 95
* Photocopiable Punctuation Unit 5, Resource 2: Pet names, page 96

Additional resources
* Texts containing names

Introduction

Teaching overview
This unit introduces children to the concept that we use capital letters at the start of people's names. Use the content of this unit to actively develop children's oral vocabulary as well as their ability to understand and use the grammatical structures, giving particular support to children whose oral language skills are insufficiently developed. When modelling the teaching point, use your voice to show emphasis, intonation, tone, volume and natural speech patterns. This will help beginner learners to bridge the gaps between spoken and written vocabulary, grammar and punctuation.

Introduce the concept
On the board, write: 'We went to the shop with polly.' Ask: 'Have I written a sentence?' Pause to allow the

children to think and then take suggestions. Establish that this is a sentence. Ask: 'Is everything in my sentence correct?' Agree that there is one error in it. Ask the children if they can spot what the error is in the sentence. Agree that the name 'Polly' begins with a lower-case 'p', but it should start with a capital 'P'. Invite a volunteer to come to the front and correct your sentence. Tell the children that all names need to start with a capital letter. Repeat the activity with the sentence 'Marcus ran faster than Faisal.' Ensure the children recognise and capitalise both names. Invite children to come to the board to write their names and show their classmates that they use a capital letter at the start.

Read and point to the teaching point in the Pupil Book: 'We use a capital letter at the start of a name. We still use a capital letter at the start of a sentence.'

Pupil practice

Pupil Book pages 38–39

Get started
The children copy sentences, then find and underline the capital letters. You may wish to support the children by reading each sentence aloud, then pausing while they find and point to the capital letters, before asking them to copy the sentences.

Answers
1. *We got the book for Mark.*   [example]
2. She did art with Jorge.   [2 marks]
3. Jon and Kim did maths with Klaus.   [3 marks]
4. Mum took Sally and me to the park.   [2 marks]
5. A letter arrived for Maria.   [2 marks]

Try these
The children copy and correct sentences by adding capital letters.

Answers
1. *Now Caren has a doll.*   [example]
2. Did you see how fast Eva can run?   [2 marks]
3. The cat is called Matt.   [2 marks]
4. My pet fish is called Sasha.   [2 marks]
5. Gran phoned Dan at six o'clock.   [2 marks]

Now try these

The children write three names, using a capital letter at the beginning of each name, and write three words that do not need a capital letter (unless they start a sentence).

Suggested answers

1. Accept any three names that correctly use capital letters. [3 marks]

2. Accept any three words that correctly do not use capital letters. [3 marks]

Support, embed & challenge

Support

Use Punctuation Unit 5 Resource 1: Capital letters for people's names to help these children to recognise and match capital letters with people's names. Ask the children to look at the first name. Tell them that the name 'Samira' needs a capital 'S'. Help them to find the capital 'S' and draw a line to it from the name 'Samira'. Then ask the children to match up the rest of the names with the capital letters by drawing lines. (**Answers** samira–S, mohammed–M, jane–J, charlotte–C, ben–B, alison–A, david–D, petra–P)

Embed

Use Punctuation Unit 5 Resource 2: Pet names to provide the children with practise in writing names using capital letters. Ask the children to read the worksheet and write their name ideas on the lines provided.

Challenge

Challenge these children to think about the names of characters in books. Provide them with a selection of classroom books and tell them to carry out a name hunt by looking for names and writing them down, remembering to use capital letters.

Homework / Additional activities

Family names

Ask the children to talk to their parents about the names of people in their family. Ask the children to write a list of all the people in their family, remembering to use capital letters to start the names.

Collins Connect: Punctuation Unit 2

Ask the children to complete Punctuation Unit 2 (See Teach → Year 1 → Vocabulary, Grammar and Punctuation → Punctuation Unit 2).

Note: the Collins Connect activities could be used with Unit 5 or 8.

Punctuation Unit 6: Using a capital letter for names of places

English curriculum objectives

- Using a capital letter for names of people, places, the days of the week and the personal pronoun 'I'

Treasure House resources

- Vocabulary, Grammar and Punctuation Skills Pupil Book 1, Punctuation Unit 6, pages 40–41

- Collins Connect Treasure House Vocabulary, Grammar and Punctuation Year 1, Unit 3
- Photocopiable Punctuation Unit 6, Resource 1: Place names, page 97
- Photocopiable Punctuation Unit 6, Resource 2: Fact file, page 98

Introduction

Teaching overview

This unit introduces children to the concept that we use capital letters at the start of place names. Use the content of this unit to actively develop children's oral vocabulary as well as their ability to understand and use the grammatical structures, giving particular support to children whose oral language skills are insufficiently developed. When modelling the teaching point, use your voice to show emphasis, intonation, tone, volume and natural speech patterns. This will help beginner learners to bridge the gaps between spoken and written vocabulary, grammar and punctuation.

Introduce the concept

On the board, write: 'We are going shopping in barcelona.' Do not use a capital letter for the word 'barcelona'. Ask: 'Have I written a sentence?' Pause

to allow children to think and then take suggestions. Establish that this is a sentence. Ask: 'Is my sentence correct?' Agree that there is an error in it. Ask the children if they can spot what the error is in the sentence. Establish that the name of the place 'Barcelona' begins with a lowercase 'b', but explain that place names need to start with a capital letter. Invite a volunteer to come to the front and correct your sentence. Repeat the process with the sentence 'Mum collected my sister from Oxford bus station.' Ask the children questions such as: 'Where have you been on holiday?' 'Where did you go last weekend?' 'What street is our school on?' Write the place names on the board, emphasising the capital letters.

Read and point to the teaching point in the Pupil Book: 'We use a capital letter at the start of place names. We still use a capital letter at the start of a sentence and for the names of people.'

Pupil practice

Pupil Book pages 40–41

Get started

The children copy sentences, then find and underline the capital letters. You may wish to support the children by reading each sentence aloud, then pausing while they find and point to the capital letters, before asking them to copy the sentences.

Answers

1. I live in Liverpool. [example]
2. We got the bus to London. [2 marks]
3. I went to Cambridge. [2 marks]
4. Last week we went to Switzerland. [2 marks]
5. I am going to Spain for a holiday. [2 marks]

Try these

The children copy and correct sentences by adding capital letters.

Answers

1. We used to live in New York. [example]
2. The town of Elgin is in Scotland. [3 marks]
3. We go skiing in France. [2 marks]
4. My friend lives in Texas. [2 marks]
5. There is a beach in Bournemouth. [2 marks]

Now try these

The children write three place names and then write two sentences to say where their relatives live.

Suggested answers

1. Accept any three place names that correctly use capital letters. [3 marks]
2. Accept sentences that correctly use capital letters, full stops and relevant content.
   [4 marks: 1 mark per sentence for correct punctuation, 1 mark per sentence for relevant content]

Support, embed & challenge

Support

Use Punctuation Unit 6 Resource 1: Place names to provide these children with practice in recognising, writing and discussing a selection of place names. Ask the children to read the place names and then copy each one out in the space provided, correcting it by adding a capital letter. Discuss with the children which of the place names they recognise and any experience they have of those places. (**Answers** London, Texas, Paris, France, Africa, Spain, Oxford, Wigan, America, Yorkshire)

Embed

Use Punctuation Unit 6 Resource 2: Fact file to encourage the children to think about places that are relevant to them and their experiences. Ask the children to make a fact file by answering questions about where they live, where they have been on holiday and where they would like to go. Support the children in reading the questions and considering the answers. Remind the children to use capital letters at the beginnings of the place names they write.

Challenge

Challenge these children to think some more about places that they know. Ask them to draw a map of their local area as they remember it and label it with place names. Explain that place names include the names of places such as shops, supermarkets, shopping centres, commons, parks and streets.

Homework / Additional activities

Where have you been?

Ask the children to talk to their parents about places and place names. Ask parents to help their child write a list of places they have been to locally, nationally and/or internationally.

Collins Connect: Punctuation Unit 3

Ask the children to complete Punctuation Unit 3 (See Teach → Year 1 → Vocabulary, Grammar and Punctuation → Punctuation Unit 3).

Note: the Collins Connect activities could be used with Unit 6 or 7.

Punctuation Unit 7: Using a capital letter for days of the week

Overview

English curriculum objectives
- Using a capital letter for names of people, places, the days of the week and the personal pronoun 'I'

Treasure House resources
- Vocabulary, Grammar and Punctuation Skills Pupil Book 1, Punctuation Unit 7, pages 42–43

- Collins Connect Treasure House Vocabulary, Grammar and Punctuation Year 1, Unit 3
- Photocopiable Punctuation Unit 7, Resource 1: Days of the week word search, page 99
- Photocopiable Punctuation Unit 7, Resource 2: Months of the year, page 100

Introduction

Teaching overview
This unit introduces children to the concept that we use capital letters at the start of days of the week. Use the content of this unit to actively develop children's oral vocabulary as well as their ability to understand and use the grammatical structures, giving particular support to children whose oral language skills are insufficiently developed. When modelling the teaching point, use your voice to show emphasis, intonation, tone, volume and natural speech patterns. This will help beginner learners to bridge the gaps between spoken and written vocabulary, grammar and punctuation.

Introduce the concept
On the board write: 'On sunday we have a tennis match.' Ask: Have I written a sentence? Pause to allow the children to think and then take suggestions. Establish that this is a sentence. Ask: 'Is my sentence correct?' Agree that there is an error in it. Ask the children if they can spot what the error is in the sentence. Establish that the day of the week, 'Sunday', needs to start with a capital letter. Invite a volunteer to come to the front and correct the sentence. Repeat the activity with the sentence 'I am going to the park on Friday.' Ask the children to tell you the other days of the week and, with the children's input, write them on the board, modelling the spelling and use of capital letters.

Read and point to the teaching point in the Pupil Book: 'We use a capital letter at the start of days of the week. We still use a capital letter at the start of a sentence and for the names of people and places.'

Pupil practice

Pupil Book pages 42–43

Get started
The children copy sentences, then find and underline the capital letters. You may wish to support the children by reading each sentence aloud, then pausing while they find and point to the capital letters, before asking them to copy the sentences.

Answers
1. *On Monday, we have an art lesson.* [example]
2. I must remember my gym kit on Tuesday. [2 marks]
3. The new film is showing on Wednesday. [2 marks]
4. On Thursday, my friend is coming for tea. [2 marks]
5. We will have fun on Saturday. [2 marks]

Try these
The children copy and correct the sentences by adding capital letters.

Answers
1. *We have a big day on Tuesday.* [example]

2. It is a fact that Friday is the day after Thursday. [3 marks]
3. Friday is the day we eat fish and chips. [1 mark]
4. We are going shopping on Saturday. [2 marks]
5. I like Monday the best. [2 marks]

Now try these
The children write the days of the week and write two sentences about what they do on different days of the week.

Suggested answers
1. Monday, Tuesday, Wednesday, Thursday, Friday, Saturday, Sunday. [7 marks]
2. Accept sentences that correctly use capital letters, full stops and relevant content.
[4 marks: 1 mark per sentence for correct punctuation, 1 mark per sentence for relevant content]

Support, embed & challenge

Support

Use Punctuation Unit 7 Resource 1: Days of the week word search to provide these children with practice in recognising, reading and writing the days of the week. Ask the children to find the days of the week in the word search, then write each day in its correct place on the list underneath.

(**Answers**

m	t	u	e	s	d	a	y	g	p
o	f	e	s	u	n	d	a	y	s
n	r	l	d	i	v	k	y	h	k
d	i	t	h	u	r	s	d	a	y
a	d	m	c	r	o	s	e	x	t
y	a	s	a	t	u	r	d	a	y
f	y	b	q	n	z	r	j	u	w
w	e	d	n	e	s	d	a	y	a

Monday, Tuesday, Wednesday, Thursday, Friday, Saturday, Sunday)

Embed

Use Punctuation Unit 7 Resource 2: Months of the year to introduce the children to the fact that the months of the year also need capital letters (thereby further developing the idea that all proper nouns need a capital letter). Ask the children to read the months, then copy them out using capital letters at the beginning of each. You could also ask the children to cut out the words, jumble them up and then reorder them correctly to practise putting them in the correct order. (**Answers** January, February, March, April, May, June, July, August, September, October, November, December)

Challenge

Ask these children to think about what happens on different days of the week, for example what day their PE lesson is on or which day is their favourite. Challenge them to write sentences about the days of the week.

Homework / Additional activities

Days of the week

Ask the children to talk to their parents about the days of the week. Ask parents to describe to their child what they do on each day of the week, for example which days they go shopping, which days they do the ironing. Ask them to support their children in writing a basic calendar for the week.

Collins Connect: Punctuation Unit 3

Ask the children to complete Punctuation Unit 3 (See Teach → Year 1 → Vocabulary, Grammar and Punctuation → Punctuation Unit 3).

Note: the Collins Connect activities could be used with Unit 6 or 7.

Punctuation Unit 8:
Using a capital letter for 'I'

Overview

English curriculum objectives

- Using a capital letter for names of people, places, the days of the week, and the personal pronoun 'I'

Treasure House resources

- Vocabulary, Grammar and Punctuation Skills Pupil Book 1, Punctuation Unit 8, pages 44–45

- Collins Connect Treasure House Vocabulary, Grammar and Punctuation Year 1, Unit 2
- Photocopiable Punctuation Unit 8, Resource 1: Using a capital I, page 101
- Photocopiable Punctuation Unit 8, Resource 2: All about me, page 102

Introduction

Teaching overview

This unit introduces children to the concept that we use a capital letter for the personal pronoun 'I' to write about ourselves. Use the content of this unit to actively develop children's oral vocabulary as well as their ability to understand and use the grammatical structures, giving particular support to children whose oral language skills are insufficiently developed. When modelling the teaching point, use your voice to show emphasis, intonation, tone, volume and natural speech patterns. This will help beginner learners to bridge the gaps between spoken and written vocabulary, grammar and punctuation.

Introduce the concept

On the board, write: 'Today i went to the cinema.' Ask: 'Have I written a sentence?' Pause to allow the children to think and then take suggestions. Establish that this is a sentence. Ask: 'Is my sentence correct?' Agree that there is an error in it. Ask the children if they can spot what the error is in the sentence. Establish that, when we write about ourselves, we need to use a capital letter for 'I'. Invite a volunteer to come to the front and correct your sentence. Repeat the process with the sentence 'Can I have a glass of milk?' Invite the children to tell you things about themselves, such as their age, their likes and dislikes, things they do and things they have. Write their responses on the board, emphasising the capitalisation of the personal pronoun 'I'.

Read and point to the teaching point in the Pupil Book: 'We use a capital letter for the word 'I' when we write about ourselves. We still use a capital letter at the start of a sentence, for names, place names and days of the week.'

Pupil practice

Pupil Book pages 44–45

Get started

The children copy sentences, then find and underline the capital letters. You may wish to support the children by reading each sentence aloud, then pausing while they find and point to the capital letters, before asking them to copy the sentences.

Answers

1. <u>After</u> this, <u>I</u> will go swimming.   [example]
2. <u>Then</u> <u>I</u> can see <u>S</u>amira.   [3 marks]
3. <u>I</u> am having a party tomorrow.   [1 mark]
4. <u>In</u> the evening, <u>I</u> read to my mum.   [2 marks]
5. <u>Sometimes</u> <u>I</u> am very loud!   [2 marks]

Try these

The children copy and correct the sentences by adding capital letters.

Answers

1. *It is a fact that I like frogs.*   [example]
2. Mum said that I sing like a pop star.   [2 marks]
3. Can I have an apple?   [2 marks]
4. In the mornings, I get ready for school.   [2 marks]
5. I have a new backpack.   [1 mark]

Now try these

The children write two sentences about themselves, using the personal pronoun 'I' and then write three words that do not need capital letters (unless they start a sentence).

Suggested answers

1. Accept any properly formed and punctuated sentences about the child.
   [4 marks: 1 mark per sentence for the correct use of capital letters, 1 mark per sentence for relevant content]
2. Accept any three words that correctly do not use capital letters.   [3 marks]

Support, embed & challenge

Support

Use Punctuation Unit 8 Resource 1: Using a capital I to provide these children with practice in capitalising the personal pronoun 'I'. Ask the children to copy and correct the sentences by using a capital 'I' where it is needed. Support the children in reading the sentences. (**Answers** 1. I am sure I put my glasses in my bag. 2. I wonder what I will do this afternoon. 3. I had a great time and I will be back next time. 4. I moved house and I unpacked my things. 5. I am running late and I will miss my bus!)

Embed

Use Punctuation Unit 8 Resource 2: All about me to give the children the opportunity to construct their own sentences about themselves, using the personal pronoun 'I'. Read and discuss the topics with the children: colours, school, hobbies, toys, home, family, clothes, food, friends. Ask them to choose four topics from the boxes, then write a sentence about themselves using 'I' for each topic they've chosen.

Challenge

Challenge these children to imagine they are meeting a new teacher for the very first time. They want to tell the teacher all about themselves. Ask the children to write sentences using a capital 'I' to write about themselves.

Homework / Additional activities

Me, myself and I

Ask the children to talk about using a capital 'I' to refer to themselves. Ask parents to point out the personal pronoun 'I' to their children in their reading books.

Collins Connect: Punctuation Unit 2

Ask the children to complete Punctuation Unit 2 (See Teach → Year 1 → Vocabulary, Grammar and Punctuation → Punctuation Unit 2).

Note: the Collins Connect activities could be used with Unit 5 or 8.

Punctuation Unit 9:
Punctuating sentences

Overview

English curriculum objectives

- Introduction to capital letters, full stops, question marks and exclamation marks to demarcate sentences
- Using a capital letter for names of people, places, the days of the week and the personal pronoun 'I'

Treasure House resources

- Vocabulary, Grammar and Punctuation Skills Pupil Book 1, Punctuation Unit 9, pages 46–47
- Collins Connect Treasure House Vocabulary, Grammar and Punctuation Year 1, Unit 1
- Photocopiable Punctuation Unit 9, Resource 1: End of sentence punctuation, page 103
- Photocopiable Punctuation Unit 9, Resource 2: Correcting sentences, page 104

Introduction

Teaching overview

This unit consolidates and provides further practice in punctuating simple sentences correctly using capital letters and full stops, question marks or exclamation marks. Use the content of this unit to actively develop children's oral vocabulary as well as their ability to understand and use the grammatical structures, giving particular support to children whose oral language skills are insufficiently developed. When modelling the teaching point, use your voice to show emphasis, intonation, tone, volume and natural speech patterns. This will help beginner learners to bridge the gaps between spoken and written vocabulary, grammar and punctuation.

Introduce the concept

Ask the children to tell you what sentences need. Discuss and elicit suggestions such as:

- words in the correct order with spaces between them

- capital letters for the start and for people, place names, and 'I'
- a full stop, question mark or exclamation mark at the end.

Ask volunteers to suggest example sentences. Support them in writing their sentences on the board and working with the other children to check that they are correctly punctuated.

Read and point to the teaching point in the Pupil Book: 'Sentences always need a capital letter at the start. At the end, you need to put a full stop, a question mark or an exclamation mark.

- Full stop: .
- Statement: I am nine.
- Question mark: ?
- Question: Are you glad?
- Exclamation mark: !
- Exclamation: She is so funny!'

Pupil practice

Pupil Book pages 46–47

Get started

The children copy sentences, then find and underline the capital letters and draw a ring around the end punctuation. You may wish to support the children by reading each sentence aloud, then pausing while they find and point to the capital letters and end punctuation, before asking them to copy the sentences.

Answers

1. *Jamal went for a run.*   *[example]*
2. Jan tripped and fell!   [2 marks]
3. There was a blackbird in the garden.   [2 marks]
4. What did my cat do?   [2 marks]
5. My cat sat on a car.   [2 marks]

Try these

The children copy sentences, then draw a ring around the full stops, underline the question marks once and underline the exclamation marks twice.

Answers

1. *I went to see a film.*   *[example]*
2. What was it like?   [1 mark]
3. It was good.   [1 mark]
4. What happened in it?   [1 mark]
5. There was a funny clown!   [1 mark]

Now try these

The children copy and correct sentences by adding capital letters and the correct end punctuation.

You may wish to support children by discussing the task before setting them to work independently or in pairs.

Answers

1. Can you skip?   [2 marks]

2. I like books.   [2 marks]

3. A shark is in my pond!   [2 marks]

Support, embed & challenge

Support

Use Punctuation Unit 9 Resource 1: End of sentence punctuation to help the children to think more about which end punctuation to use. Read each sentence aloud to the children and use your voice intonation to emphasise whether the sentence is a question or exclamation. Ask the children to tick the correct type of end punctuation (question mark or exclamation mark) for each sentence. (**Answers** 1. Wait, don't leave without me [!] 2. Are you hungry [?] 3. What a horrible, wet and rainy day [!] 4. I hate the colour pink [!] 5. Do you like the colour pink [?] 6. Oh no, he has dropped pink paint everywhere [!])

Embed

Use Punctuation Unit 9 Resource 2: Correcting sentences to provide the children with the opportunity to consolidate their knowledge of sentence punctuation. Support the children in reading the sentences and prompt them to think about which words in each sentence need capital letters and which end punctuation each sentence needs. Then ask the children to copy the sentences on the lines provided, correcting each sentence by using capital letters and adding end punctuation. (**Answers** 1. Monday comes before Tuesday and Wednesday. 2. Verity jumped when she saw a huge spider. 3. How did Horace get up that tree? 4. We are going to London on the train in February. 5. I live in Basingstoke in Hampshire. 6. Where has Timothy gone? [Accept exclamation marks in place of full stops.])

Challenge

Challenge these children to make a poster that could be displayed in the classroom telling writers everything they need to remember about sentence punctuation. The posters could be created in pairs or groups.

Homework / Additional activities

What's in a sentence?

Ask the children to talk with their parents about the things sentences need. Ask them to find other examples of punctuation marks that occur in the middle of sentences and ask their parents to note them down on a piece of paper so the children can bring them to school and show the class.

Collins Connect: Punctuation Unit 1

Ask the children to complete Punctuation Unit 1 (See Teach → Year 1 → Vocabulary, Grammar and Punctuation → Punctuation Unit 1).

Review unit 3: Punctuation

A. The children copy and correct the sentences by adding spaces between the words.

Answers

1. The baby was shaking a rattle.   [1 mark]

2. It is a cold day.   [1 mark]

3. The car horn beeped.   [1 mark]

4. I saw a big spider.   [1 mark]

B. The children copy and correct sentences by adding capital letters.

Answers

1. Waheed wanted to sit next to Tyler.   [2 marks]

2. We went on a trip to Newcastle.   [2 marks]

3. I am saving my pocket money.   [1 mark]

4. Tuesday is the day after Monday.   [2 marks]

C. The children copy and correct sentences by adding the end punctuation.

Answers

1. Quick, stop that thief!   [1 mark]

2. Are you hungry?   [1 mark]

3. I have finished my work.   [1 mark]

4. What time is it?   [1 mark]

D. The children write a question of their own construction.

[3 marks: 1 mark for the correct use of capital letters, 1 mark for the correct use of a question mark and 1 mark for relevant content]

E. The children write an exclamation of their own construction.

[3 marks: 1 mark for the correct use of capital letters, one mark for the correct use of an exclamation mark and one mark for relevant content]

Adding –s

Do you need to add the suffix **–s** in the gap?
Tick 'yes' if you do or 'no' if you don't.
Add the suffix **–s** if you ticked **yes**. One has been done for you.

	yes	no
I saw three swan_s_ on the lake.	✓	
There are two pillow__ on my bed.		
Three cat__ live next door to me.		
Mum gave me a new pencil__.		
I picked four apple__.		

Plural nouns with the suffix –s

Write the missing word. Then draw the pictures.
One has been done for you.

one spoon	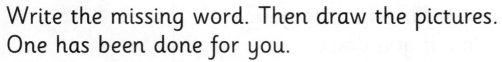	two spoons	
one frog		three _____	
one bird		four _____	
one car		five _____	
one flower		six _____	

Singular nouns and plural nouns ending –es

Do these words mean one thing or more than one thing?
Tick 'singular' for words that mean one thing or 'plural' for words that mean more than one thing. One has been done for you.

	singular	plural		singular	plural
fox	✓		wish		
benches			kisses		
bushes			foxes		
box			bush		
dishes			boxes		
bench			quiz		
bus			dish		
watches			kiss		

Using words ending –es

Continue the story using the words in the box.
Then draw a picture of your story.

| two foxes   two dishes   two boxes   some bushes   three wishes |

Once upon a time there were two little foxes called...

_____

_____

_____

_____

_____

_____

_____

Adding –ing to verbs

Read the word sums and write the new words.
One has been done for you.

1. milk + ing = <u>*milking*</u>

2. draw + ing = _____

3. sleep + ing = _____

4. talk + ing = _____

5. ask   + ing = _____

6. think + ing = _____

7. meet + ing = _____

8. throw + ing = _____

Using verbs ending –ing

Fill the gap in each sentence.
Choose the correct word from the box.
Write it in the gap.

> climbing   reading   throwing   watching
> drawing   catching   laughing

1. We had fun _____ the tree.

2. The film kept us _____ all day.

3. The teacher was _____ a story.

4. I enjoyed _____ a picture.

5. He was _____ the show.

6. We were _____ and _____ the ball.

Adding –ed to verbs

Read the word sums and write the new words.
One has been done for you.

1. show + ed = <u>showed</u>

2. look + ed = _____

3. count + ed = _____

4. pick + ed = _____

5. ask + ed = _____

6. press + ed = _____

7. answer + ed = _____

8. clean + ed = _____

Past or future tense?

Read each sentence and tick a box to say whether
it happened in the past or whether it hasn't happened yet.

	It happened in the past.	It hasn't happened yet.
1. I jumped into the mud.	☐	☐
2. I will jump into the mud.	☐	☐
3. I finished tidying my bedroom.	☐	☐
4. I will finish tidying my bedroom.	☐	☐
5. I coloured the picture.	☐	☐
6. I am going to colour the picture.	☐	☐

Using adjectives to compare

Write the final word in each sentence.
One has been done for you.

1. Annie's sunflower is tall but Emma's sunflower is <u>taller</u>_____.

2. Zain can run fast but Harry can run _____.

3. My lamp is bright but the sun is _____.

4. The days are cold but the nights are _____.

5. Your grandpa is old but mine is _____.

6. A mouse is small but a bee is even _____.

About me

Complete these sentences to make them true for you.
For each sentence, choose an adjective from the box
and write it in the first gap. Then write the name of a person or a
thing in the second gap.

| taller   shorter   younger   older |

1. I am _____ than _____ .

2. I am _____ than _____ .

3. I am _____ than _____ .

4. I am _____ than _____ .

Think of two adjectives of your own and complete these sentences.

5. I am _____ than _____ .

6. I am _____ than _____ .

Rosettes

Award each rosette to a person you know that matches the description. Write their name in the middle. One has been done for you.

To the oldest person I know

To the tallest person I know

To the cleanest person I know

To the loudest person I know

To the smartest person I know

To the youngest person I know

Labels

Use the words in the box to label the items.

highest smallest largest lightest lowest darkest tallest shortest

_____ _____ _____

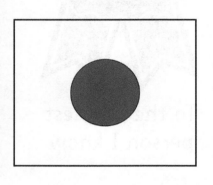 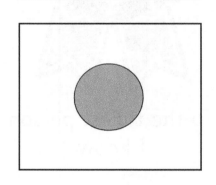 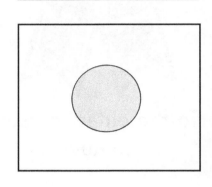

_____ _____ _____

 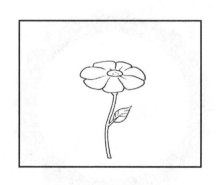 

_____ _____ _____

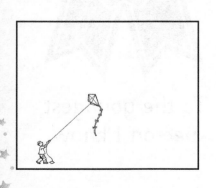 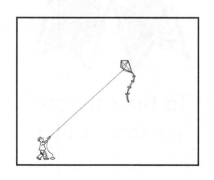 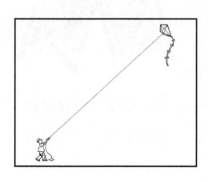

_____ _____ _____

Adding un–

Read the word sums and write the new words.
One has been done for you.

1. un + fair = *unfair*

2. un + lock = _____

3. un + do = _____

4. un + hook = _____

5. un + afraid = _____

6. un + load = _____

7. un + paid = _____

8. un + lit = _____

Word search

Find the words that begin with **un–** in the word search.

unfit undress unblock unstick unlit unpack unpaid unafraid

u	n	a	f	r	a	i	d
n	u	n	s	t	i	c	k
d	a	j	d	o	e	u	u
r	u	n	l	i	t	n	n
e	g	k	h	b	f	p	p
s	u	n	f	i	t	a	a
s	c	n	p	l	m	c	i
u	n	b	l	o	c	k	d

Making sentences

Cut out the words.
Put them in the right order to make sentences.

the	at	children
played	The	park.

dug	rabbit	deep
The	a	burrow.

wind.	in	The
kite	the	flew

Building your own sentences

Cut out the words.
Choose words to build your own sentences.

The	cat	with
ate	tricked	a
monkey	song	hid
an	the	sang
horse	pushed	parrot
mouse	played	happy

Is it a sentence?

Read each line.
Tick 'yes' if it is a sentence and 'no' if it is not a sentence.

	yes	no
1. I hair my brushed.	☐	☐
2. We had soup for lunch.	☐	☐
3. Pen my is blue.	☐	☐
4. Today sunny is a day.	☐	☐
5. I packed my bag.	☐	☐
6. We had yes and.	☐	☐
7. You are my best friend.	☐	☐
8. Like I fish chips and.	☐	☐

Finishing sentences

Finish each sentence.

1. This morning I _____

_____

2. On the way to school I _____

_____

3. When I got to school I _____

_____

4. I like to play _____

_____

5. My friends are called _____

_____

6. For lunch I have _____

_____

Joining sentences

Draw lines to join the sentence parts together.
Look for the topics that match.

I like yellow and   your hair is short.

I count to ten and   I like to drink juice.

My hair is long and   I like red.

It is a hot day and   you count to twenty.

I like to play cars and   I like to play trains.

I like to drink milk and   I would like an ice-cream.

Building sentences using 'and'

Cut out the words. Put them in the right order
to make sentences that use the word 'and'.

we	is	cold.
are	and	snowing
It		

running	I	I
and	like	like
hopping.		

Is it a sentence?

Read each line.
Tick 'yes' if it is a sentence and 'no' if it is
not a sentence.

	yes	no
1. I brush my hair I brush my teeth	☐	☐
2. We had salad and we had chips.	☐	☐
3. I have a red pen and I have a pink pen.	☐	☐
4. I am going to shop I am going to park	☐	☐
5. I put on my coat and I put on my shoes.	☐	☐
6. The pirates read the map and found the treasure.	☐	☐
7. Sam tidied his room did his homework	☐	☐
8. We are chatting listening to music	☐	☐

Completing sentences using 'but'

You can use the word 'and' to link two sentences together. Did you know you can also use the word 'but' to link two sentences? Write the word 'but' in the gaps then read the sentences.

1. I am hot _____ I don't want to take off my coat.

2. I like playing cars _____ I like playing with blocks more.

3. I have a friend called Bob _____ I also have a friend called Peter.

4. I am good at counting _____ I am not good at adding.

5. I like rabbits _____ I do not like cats.

Word snakes

How many words can you find in the word snakes?
Circle the words that you find.

1.

oneabtwocdthreeeffourghfiveij

2.

klredmnyellowmnblueopgreengrorange

3.

doghtcatuvmouseghbirdzahorsebc

4.

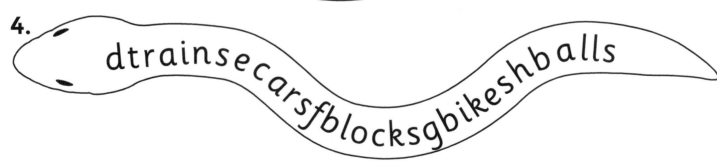

dtrainsecarsfblocksgbikeshballs

Spaces between words

Correct each sentence by adding spaces.
Practise using different sized spaces until you find a
size that looks right.

1. Thesheepweregrazing.

_____

2. Thehenswereclucking.

_____

3. Thedogwasbarking.

_____

4. Thecowswereeating.

_____

5. Thefarmerwasdigging.

_____

Matching letters

Draw lines to match the capital letters to the lowercase letters.

a	e	M	q
b	D	n	p
C	B	O	Z
d	k	P	o
E	F	Q	v
f	I	r	m
G	J	s	R
H	L	T	N
i	A	U	t
j	h	V	X
K	g	W	w
l	c	x	y
		Y	S
		z	u

Writing capital letters

Write the correct capital letter next to each lowercase letter.

a	A	b	
c		d	
e		f	
g		h	
i		j	
k		l	
m		n	
o		p	
q		r	
s		t	
u		v	
w		x	
y		z	

Adding question marks

Read each sentence.
If it is a question, add a question mark at the end.
If it is not a question, add a full stop at the end.

1. Have you been busy today ☐

2. I am tired ☐

3. Can you hop on one foot ☐

4. Are you feeling happy ☐

5. I need a drink ☐

6. What day is it ☐

7. I like reading ☐

8. Do you like reading ☐

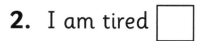

Matching questions and answers

Draw lines to match the questions to the answers.

1. What colour is a carrot?

a. I am six years old.

2. What time is it?

b. my teddy

3. How old are you?

c. orange

4. What is your favourite food?

d. It is two o'clock.

5. What day is it tomorrow?

e. I love pasta.

6. What is your favourite toy?

f. Thursday

Adding exclamation marks and question marks

Read each sentence and decide whether it is a question or an exclamation. If it is an exclamation, add an exclamation mark at the end. If it is a question, add a question mark at the end.

1. How dreadful

2. Is it three o'clock yet

3. What a terrible noise

4. How very embarrassing

5. What would you like to drink

6. Are we nearly there yet

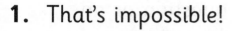

Exclamations

Draw lines to match the exclamations to the pictures.

1. That's impossible! **a.**

2. I'm covered in mud! **b.**

3. We found the treasure! **c.**

4. Help, I'm stuck! **d.**

5. The house burned down! **e.**

Capital letters for people's names

Draw lines to match the correct capital letter to each name.

samira   C

mohammed   P

jane   D

charlotte   S

ben   J

alison   M

david   A

petra   B

Pet names

These children have got new pets.
They need your help to think of names.
Write your idea for a name in each space.

1. Clara got a cat. Give it a name: _____

2. Freddie got a fish. Give it a name: _____

3. Henry got a horse. Give it a name: _____

4. Tamir got a terrapin. Give it a name: _____

5. Sophie got a spider. Give it a name: _____

Place names

Here are lots of place names.
Copy them out correctly using capital letters
to start them. How many of these places have you heard of?

Place name	Copy it here	Place name	Copy it here
london		texas	
paris		france	
africa		spain	
oxford		wigan	
america		yorkshire	

Fact file

Make a fact file about places you know.
Answer each question and remember to use capital letters.

1. Which country do you live in?

_____

2. Which city, town or village do you live in?

_____

3. Which street do you live in?

_____

4. Where in the world have you been on holiday?

_____

5. Where in the world would you like to go?

_____

Days of the week word search

Find the days of the week in the word search.
Then write them on the lines provided.

m	t	u	e	s	d	a	y	g	p
o	f	e	s	u	n	d	a	y	s
n	r	l	d	i	v	k	y	h	k
d	i	t	h	u	r	s	d	a	y
a	d	m	c	r	o	s	g	z	t
y	a	s	a	t	u	r	d	a	y
f	y	b	q	n	z	r	j	u	w
w	e	d	n	e	s	d	a	y	a

M_____ F_____

T_____ S_____

W_____ S_____

T_____

Months of the year

The months of the year also need a capital letter at the start. Copy each month, but use a capital letter to correctly start each month.

january	
february	
march	
april	
may	
june	
july	
august	
september	
october	
november	
december	

Using a capital I

Copy and correct these sentences by using a capital
I where it is needed.

1. i am sure i put my glasses in my bag.

    _____

2. i wonder what i will do this afternoon.

    _____

3. i had a great time and i will be back next time.

    _____

4. i moved house and i unpacked my things.

    _____

5. i am running late and i will miss my bus!

    _____

All about me

Choose four topics from the boxes.
Write a sentence about yourself using 'I' for each
topic you choose.

colours	school	hobbies
toys	home	family
clothes	food	friends

_____

_____

_____

_____

_____

_____

_____

_____

End of sentence punctuation

Tick the correct type of end punctuation for each sentence.

	!	?
1. Wait, don't leave without me	☐	☐
2. Are you hungry	☐	☐
3. What a horrible, wet and rainy day	☐	☐
4. I hate the colour pink	☐	☐
5. Do you like the colour pink	☐	☐
6. Oh no, he has dropped pink paint everywhere	☐	☐

Correcting sentences

Copy and correct these sentences by adding capital letters and end punctuation.

1. monday comes before tuesday and wednesday

   _____

2. verity jumped when she saw a huge spider

   _____

3. how did horace get up that tree

   _____

4. we are going to london on the train in february

   _____

5. i live in basingstoke in hampshire

   _____

6. where has timothy gone

   _____